PLANTS & FLOWERS
for
HOME & GARDEN

Marshall Cavendish

Photo credits

Harry Smith
Valerie Finnis
P. Genereux
Peter Hunt
K. A. Beckett
Violet Stevenson
R. J. Corbin
Iris Hardwick
Dennis Woodland
John Banks
D. C. Arminson
Ray Procter
Elsa M. Megson
Leslie Johns
C. Dawson
G. Hyde
D. Wildridge
Ianthe Ruthven
G. Rodway
Pamela Booth
P. Ayres
A. J. Huxley
R. J. Corbin
A. Rainbow
W. J. Tjaden
D. J. Kesby
Carlo Bevilacqua
Ruth Rutter
Amateur Gardening
H. R. Hood
J. E. Downward
Edna Knowles
Henry J. Wood
John Markham
John Hovell
Picturepoint
A. Boarder
Sheila J. Orme
F. W. Buglass
Mondadori Press
Tourist Photo Library
B. G. Furner
National Botanic Garden of South Africa
Maurice Nimmo
A. D. Schilling
T. R. M. Lothian
N. Chaffer
Slide Centre

CONTENTS

Published by Marshall Cavendish Books Limited
58 Old Compton Street
London W1V 5PA

Printed and bound in Hong Kong by Dai Nippon
Printing Company

ISBN 0 85685 015 2

Modern methods and machinery have ensured that gardening need no longer be a back-breaking, muscle-cracking slog. Here is a book which shows how — with minimum effort — anyone can grow beautiful, fragrant flowers to enhance the garden and decorate the home.

People naturally enjoy transforming a house into a home, furnishing it with comfort, decorating it with ornaments they choose, embroidering and embellishing it with the colours they favour. And this has always been so—even in the caves of primitive man. But today a garden—truly a frame for a well-run and beautiful home—is becoming more and more an extension of the home and people are tending to regard it as such.

And so it is that rows of regimented vivid scarlets, bright oranges and yellows are being quietly superseded by softer hues—by pinks, lavender, blue, grey, silver and even those kind, green flowers. Handsome foliage, the furniture of the garden, is as much appreciated as beautiful furnishings in the home. And successful gardening need not be hard work. Today is the perfect age for 'effortless gardening', especially now that modern

machinery and methods have taken much of the hard, muscle-cracking slog out of gardening. Mowing the lawn, trimming the edges, clipping hedges, dull work, is often quickly done with the aid of electrical appliances—hardly more laborious than vacuuming and dusting the house. People who enjoy gentle gardening are generally more interested in ends than in means. The aim for most of them is to grow plants for beauty, for flowers to cut, for

fragrance, for fun, without a lot of hard work. They feel that a garden should be full of interest and delight, not full of demanding, never ending chores.

This book recognises this and begins with the fundamental advice on how to make gardens easy to run as well as good to look at. Certain plants can serve the gardener as well as decorate the scene. It is important to know which to grow.

Judging by my mailbag, what most people want from their garden is to have something to admire, to wonder at, to cut, to look at from the house when they are busy within, a visual refreshment at times of the year. This is possible and this book will help them decide what to grow and how to grow it. Many people dream of seeing their homes wreathed in lovely undemanding climbers, honeysuckle over the windowsills, fences softened and even made beautiful by evergreen and floral drapes, unsightly sheds hidden by cascading blossom or a garage wall offering a home for fragrant roses. What is not generally appreciated is that by growing plants against any vertical surface, the area of actual garden is greatly increased, a practice which should be encouraged. Many climbers are both easy and spectacular. Some provide flowers for cutting.

One of the great maxims for gardeners used to be that for easy, successful gardening, one ought to

stay with plants indigenous to the local soil. Since soils vary considerably and since one can waste one's time and the life of a cherished plant by trying to force it to accept the wrong environment this seems good advice.

But many gardeners on other soils envy those who garden on acid, peaty land, who can colour their plots with flamboyant rhododendrons and ground-covering heathers and other calcifuges, all of them requiring so little attention yet producing wonderful colour effects, some of them even in mid-winter. I garden on lime soil yet I have all these plants by making special raised borders, using peat bricks as 'walls' and more peat for planting. Anyone on any soil can grow peat-loving plants and so take full advantage of their amiable nature. Meanwhile, of course, the main part of the garden can still be reserved for plants which are happy with the local soil conditions and climate.

Those who garden on chalk need special help. There are many lovely plants which will grow splendidly in such gardens. Other problems to be dealt with are those of shade and seaside gardens, all of which have special plants to suit them. Fortunately, there are scented flowers and plants for every type of soil and since most people love these I have found much to say about flowers for fragrance.

The garden should be an extension of the house and what better link than a patio distinctively and attractively furnished with plants

leading from one to the other? There is a great variety that can be grown successfully and prettily in many kinds of containers. So many people have green fingers and could easily coax and induce a mass of flowers from a few plants —a potted flower show. This is yet another way in which one can increase the area of the garden, for baskets cascading with flowers and attractive foliage can hang overhead, windowsills can spill over with summer-long flowers and winter evergreens—greys or golds. There are sink and miniature gardens of many kinds for those who lose their hearts to the tiny doll's house proportions of alpine plants. Indoors, windowsill plants ensure some flower new every morning. About the home and for any room, there are longer-lived, evergreen plants, horticultural pets, which breathe life into the surroundings and provide companionship. You are never alone with a plant.

Flower arrangement is an ideal opportunity to decorate the home with flair and at the same time it offers a medium of creative self-expression. People interested in this gentle domestic art, will want to know what leaves, flowers, fruits and seedheads grow best. They will want to know how to dry and preserve them for beautiful long-lasting winter arrangements. They will want to know which are the most profitable plants to grow for cut-and-come-again flowers for spring and summer arrangements. All this information and much more is here—just read on!

CHAPTER ONE
EASY GARDENING

One of the best ways of ensuring an informal garden is to choose plants which will work for you. The most important of these are known as ground covering plants. But ground-covering plants bring not only the suppression of weeds and the conserving of moisture and fertility: they also are flowering plants in their own right, and contribute to the garden scene through the year, providing the lowly and diverse greenery that is needed to make effective contrast and texture to that of the shrubs. Even so, while they are mostly flowering plants, few of them flower for more than a few weeks and their foliage is, therefore, particularly valuable.

The perennials, evergreen (marked *) or deciduous fall into three categories: (a) those which spread freely by underground roots, (b) those which run freely on the surface, and (c) those which are clump forming, relying upon division for their increase. Examples:

(a) *Convallaria majalis, Asperula odorata, Cerastium tomentosum;*

(b) *Vinca minor*, Stachys lanata, Tiarella cordifolia, Waldsteinia ternata*, Asarum europaeum*, Polygonum affine;*

(c) *Brunnera macrophylla,* epimedium, *Geranium macrorrhizum, G. renardii, G. ibericum platyphyllum, G. endressii,* pulmonaria, tellima*, *Stachys macrantha, Alchemilla mollis, Phlomis russelliana.*

In fact I have to begin with a word of warning. These plants are so ready to romp away that some have to be controlled.

Cerastium This genus has some undeniably attractive species with masses of small white flowers above a mat of grey leaves, but nearly all are very invasive and will ramp anywhere in any soil, so caution should be exercised before introducing plants which may soon become weeds, in spite of their beauty. They are useful for covering difficult banks, particularly by a riverside which are too steep for grass and need binding as a precaution against floods.

Also easy going are the many plants which grow in attractive masses both high

1 *Prunus pissardii* grown as a standard in the cottage garden at Penshurst Place, Kent
2 The pink-flowered *Geranium dalmaticum*
3 *Geranium psilostemon,* the most startling magenta with black centre
Here the golden leaves of
4 *Lysimachia nummularia aurea* quickly spread over the surrounding paving stones
5 *Cerastium tomentosum* called, Snow-in-Summer because of the white flowers produced in June on 6 inch stems. Easy to grow, this is popular with new gardeners

and lowly and we shall learn more of these later. The following is an example.

Geranium (jer-ay-ne-um)
From the Greek *geranos,* a crane, because the seed pod resembles a crane's head and beak (*Geraniaceae*). Crane's-bill. A genus of hardy herbaceous summer-flowering perennials with lobed or cut leaves, widely distributed over the temperate regions of the world. They are easily cultivated, free flowering, and some are useful rock garden plants, others good border plants.

Varieties of *Hedera helix,* the common ivy, are also good for shady banks, but take some years to create an impenetrable carpet. *Luzula maxima* is an ideal substitute for shady banks where grass mowing is difficult, and thrives best in cool,

Ferns make good ground covers in shady situations. For dry shade use Dryopteris felix mas and various polystichums. In moist situations plant Onoclea sensibilis

Ground covering plants suppress weeds and conserve both moisture and fertility

4

5

moist districts. The most difficult positions to cover are found under big trees such as elms, beeches and cedars. Few plants will grow under the first two; but *Hedera helix hibernica* usually succeeds if the tree branches are high. Under cedars and other trees *Cyclamen neapolitanum* will establish itself, particularly on limy soils; an annual which will thrive in the same conditions is *Oxalis rosea*. For almost any position in sun or shade, on chalk or light or heavy soils, *Hypericum calycinum* will be successful, while for really small borders many of the mat-forming rock plants are without peer, such as *Dryas sundermannii*, antennaria, acaena, cotula, ajuga, 'mossy' saxifrages, *Hypericum rhodopaeum*, and

many of these are suitable as anti-splash plants for small bulbs.

If you are interested in flower arrangement you will find so many of these plants useful.

Alchemilla, for instance, is a great favourite. When grown on the rock garden, it is best planted in crevices between rocks. *A. mollis,* 12 inches, attractive, with kidney-shaped, wavy-edged, softly hairy leaves and greenish-yellow flowers, good for cutting. Contrasts well when grown in association with *Campanula poscharskyana*. Inclined to be invasive when established, but well worth growing, especially as ground cover in shady or semi-shady places, such as under trees.

This is just one of many lovely foliage plants which are easy to grow.

Although green predominates, many plants have beautifully shaped or marked leaves. *Acanthus spinosus*, for instance, has leaves about a foot in length, deeply divided and spiny and a deep, steely green that is almost grey. Some plants, such as the ivies, provide two different kinds of foliage, one on the young plant and the mature foliage. In *Alchemilla mollis*, the lady's mantle, and its dainty relative *A. alpina*, the young leaves are pleated like a fan, and if sprayed with water hold silver drops, as they are covered with downy hairs. The true geraniums (cranebills) are all very easily grown;

1

Alchemilla flowers will dry well for winter decorations. Cut the flowers when they are just mature, hang head down in small bunches in a warm, dark place until dry

If you like butterflies in the garden plant Sedum spectabile, which they visit for the nectar of its late-blooming flowers

Geranium phaeum, and *G. ibericum* (hairy as well) provide especially good foliage, while the leaves of *G. macrorrhizum* colour well in the autumn. More perennials, the backbone of all good gardens to provide good green leaves, are the hellebores, particularly the handsome *Helleborus argutifolius (H. corsicus)* which provides formidably spined dark, glossy leaves all the year round.

For a waxy texture the fleshy oval leaves of *Sedum spectabile* are hard to rival. Woolly-leaved plants usually like the sun, so choose the sunniest spot to get the best results with the evergreen *Ballota pseudodictamnus* which makes whippy branches with small round woolly

1 *Alchemilla mollis*, **the Lady's Mantle, bears delicate flowers and is a ground cover plant for shady situations**
2 Cineraria, euphorbia and senecio make striking contrasts in this town garden
3 Island borders, an up-to-date idea, can be looked at from all sides
4 Spring in a cottage garden when colour is provided with wallflowers, violas and alpines easily grown on a retaining wall

3

2

4

leaves along their length. *Olearia mollis*, an attractive daisy bush, and its larger relative, *O. semidentata*, both have truly white woolly leaves. Soft white foliage comes on *Santolina chamaecyparissus* and *S. neopolitana*, the cotton lavenders, particularly on the latter, and both make a good low dividing line between flower border and vegetable garden. Try also *Anaphalis triplinervis* and *A. margaritacea* for double value; they have grey-white leaves in soft sprays and white 'everlasting' daisies.

The artemisias provide soft plumes of silvery foliage. *A. absinthium* is almost frothy in effect, particularly the form 'Lambrook Silver'. *A. ludoviciana* and *A.* 'Silver Queen' both have good filigree foliage leaves which individually press beautifully. The architectural plants par excellence for white woolly foliage are the biennial *Onopordon arabicum* up to 8 or 10 feet.

Although it is important to stake certain herbaceous perennials there are many others which are self-supporting, so choose these wherever possible. You might like to grow them in island borders.

If you like waist-high gardening consider establishing raised beds in certain parts of the garden.

Paving stones, set in the ground on

1 The dark purple flowers of *Geranium phaeum*, Mourning Widow
2 Buxton's Blue is a fine variety of *Geranium wallichianum*
3 Raised beds can be made to grow any type of plant
4 Herbaceous borders composed of perennial plants provide colour and interest. Staking can be reduced by planting self supporting up-to-date cultivars

1

3

edge to form a square or rectangle filled with good soil, make delightful, small raised gardens where space is limited. Not only can the surface soil be filled with colourful plants, but the vertical space between the slabs offers an excellent site for trailing plants, such as alpine phlox, aubrietas, thymes, sempervivums (house-leeks) and various campanulas.

The top of the bed may be planted with unusual bulbs, such as those of South African origin which require very sharp drainage. Dwarf conifers and rare alpine plants which dislike winter wet may also be planted, and will be seen to better advantage.

For lime-hating plants a raised peat bed supported by peat walls, is attractive in appearance and easy to plant. The peat blocks for such a wall should be not less than 12 inches long by 8 inches wide and 6 inches deep, and are laid in the same manner as bricks, using peat litter or leaf soil in place of mortar. The peat blocks must be moist when laid, so if they are delivered in a dry state, they must be immersed in a tub of water before being placed in position. Also, a peat wall should be in partial shade, because in a sunny position it would require constant watering in summer to keep the peat moist. The peat blocks should be placed sloping slightly inwards so that rainwater is retained. With a vertical wall it would drain away. Within the peat wall moist peat and leaf soil should be filled in to form a bed of a foot or more in depth. Where space permits, and there is a natural slope, raised peat beds in terraces 2 or 3 feet wide, make a charming setting for many ericaceous plants, such as gaultherias, dwarf rhododendrons, hardy heathers, also hardy ferns, ramondas, trilliums, dwarf astilbes and many other delightful hardy plants.

Cottage gardening

If you live in a cottage you can create a delightful garden to suit your home.

We cannot put the clock back, but there is no reason why the contemporary cottage garden should not reflect the old-world charm of its predecessors while making use, at the same time, of the new and improved varieties of older plants as well as some of those plants that have become more recently available.

Simplicity must always be the keynote of the well-designed cottage garden. This can be best achieved by a well-chosen mixture of suitable plants, by unpretentious design and accessories and by the use of old-fashioned climbing plants to cover walls and fences.

4

Normally, the plants are so closely packed together that weeds get little opportunity to take hold. For the contemporary cottage, grass is almost certain to play a more important part than formerly but generally speaking, the lawns will be relatively small and it should be possible to maintain it in first-rate condition at all times.

Spring Spring is a season of major interest in the cottage garden, beginning with the emergence of the snowdrops and winter aconites. The yellow buttercup-like flowers of the latter, with their attractive green ruffs, start to open during the first mild spells in January. Snowdrops, which come a little later, look best naturalised in grass. A position under old fruit trees—often to be found in the cottage garden—suits them best. Both aconites and snowdrops seed freely if left undisturbed.

These will be closely followed by the

A selection of herbaceous plants

Name	Height in feet	Colour	Season
Acanthus	4–5	lilac-pink	July–Aug
Achillea spp & vars	1–4	white, yellow	June–Aug
Alchemilla	1–1½	yellow-green	June–July
Anaphalis	1–2	white	July–Sept
Aquilegia hybs	1–3	various	May–June
Armeria	1	pinks	June–July
Artemisia	3–5	grey foliage	Aug–Sept
Aster spp & vars	1–5	various	Aug–Oct
Astrantia	2–3	green-pink	June
Bergenia	1–1½	pinks, white	March–April
Campanula	1–4	blues, white	June–Aug
Centaurea	2–5	blues, yellow	June–Oct
Cimicifuga	2–4	creamy-white	July–Sept
Coreopsis	2–3	golden-yellow	June–Sept
Corydalis	1	yellow	May–Oct
Delphinium	3–8	blues, mauves	June–July
Dianthus	½–1½	various	May–June
Dicentra	1–2	pink	April–May
Doronicum	1–2½	yellow	March–April
Echinacea	2–3	purple-red	Aug–Sept
Echinops	2–5	steely blue	July–Aug
Erigeron hybs	1–2	blue, pink	June–Sept
Eryngium	2–4	glaucous blue	July–Aug
Euphorbia	1–3	yellow	April–June
Gaillardia hybs	2	yellow, orange	July–Aug
Galega	2–4	mauve	June–July
Gentiana	1–2	blues	July–Aug
Geranium	1–2½	pinks, mauves	June–Aug
Helenium	3–5	yellows, copper	July–Sept
Hemerocallis	2–3	yellow, orange	July–Sept
Heuchera hybs	1–2½	pinks, reds	May–Aug
Iris	1–5	various	May–June
Kniphofia	1½–4	yellow, orange	July–Sept
Lupin hybs	2–4	various	June
Lythrum	2–4	purple-red	June–Sept
Lysimachia	2–4	yellow, white	July–Sept
Macleaya	5–8	apricot pink	July–Sept
Malva	2–4	mauves, pinks	July
Monarda	2–4	various	June–Aug
Nepeta	1–2	blue	May–Sept
Paeonia spp & hybs	2–4	pink, red, white	May–June
Phlox	2–4	various	July–Sept
Pyrethrum	1–3	various	May–June
Salvia spp	2–5	mauves	June–Sept
Sidalcea hybs	2½–5	pinks	June–Aug
Verbascum	3–8	yellow, pink	July–Oct
Veronica spp & vars	1–3	blues, mauves	July–Oct

Perennials for cutting

Name	Height in feet	Colour	Season
Acanthus mollis	4–5	lilac-pink	July–Aug
Achillea 'Moonshine'	2	sulphur-yellow	June–July
Alchemilla mollis	1–1½	yellowish-green	June–July
Anaphalis triplinervis	¾	white 'everlasting'	July–Aug
Aquilegia hybrids	up to 3	various	May–June
Aster (perennial)	up to 5	white, pinks, purples	Aug–Oct
Astrantia	2–3	greenish-white, pink	June
Coreopsis grandiflora	2–3	golden-yellow	June–Sep
Dianthus	½–1	various	May–June
Heuchera spp & varieties	2	pinks, reds	June–July
Iris germanica	up to 3	various	May–June
Phlox decussata	up to 3	various	July–Sep
Pyrethrum varieties	2	various	May–June
Trollius	2	yellow, gold	May–June

early daffodils and many kinds of primula.

It would seem that almost any plant with the suffix 'sweet' has affiliations with the cottage garden. Sweet peas, sweet williams, sweet sultan and sweet rocket are just a few of the cottage flowers that have earned this name, probably because fragrance plays so important a part in determining the cottager's choice of plants.

Summer As spring progresses towards summer, the cottage garden provides a continuous succession of colour and fragrance. Wallflowers, often assuming their true perennial character and coming up year after year are followed by the sweet clove-scented dianthus—the cottage pinks and clove carnations.

Here again the present-day gardener has a much wider choice where the latter plants are concerned. Interest in the old laced pinks has revived and forms are now obtainable that flower continuously throughout the summer. 'London Poppet' is white, tinged with pink and laced with ruby-red; 'Laced Hero' has large white flowers laced with purple and a central eye of chocolate-brown.

Herbs Among the major attractions of the cottage garden in summer are the fragrant herbs that provide material for sachets and *pot-pourris*, as well as for use in the kitchen. Lavender, of course, is the most widely-grown of these.

However, we shall learn a great deal more about these later on.

1 A cottage garden in Essex made colourful with hollyhocks, dahlias and salvias
2 Part of the collection of herbaceous perennials at Bressingham Hall, Norfolk, with a background of shrubs and trees
3 Bugle, helichrysum, stachys and houseleeks have a permanent foliage effect

CHAPTER TWO
A GARDEN FOR ALL SEASONS

1

2

Colour planning your garden

Nature seldom, if ever, makes mistakes with colour. Every hue seems to have full value and expression, not only to its own advantage, but also to that of the others surrounding it. Colour clashes seldom occur in nature.

Foliage has as important a part to play as flowers in garden decoration; colour variation in foliage is wide and of the utmost significance, vital to be borne in mind, especially where all-the-year-round decoration is the aim. Deciduous and evergreen leaves, therefore, should be allowed to play their full part, and not only through choice of plantings, but also by intelligent positioning in order, say, to catch the sun in certain seasons, or to match and contrast with other plantings nearby.

This applies also to the wide and vivid range of ornamental berries and barks, so useful especially during the later and winter months, when blossom is scarce.

Winter, though always a little sombre, sees many things in display: the sweetly-scented *Viburnum fragrans, Chimonanthus praecox* and *Daphne mezereum,* as examples of some lovely shrubs. *Helleborus niger,* though sometimes wayward, will offer its sheer white 'Christmas roses,' the cheerful winter aconites will shine, snowdrops need no introduction.

Over all this, the conifers and evergreens in general maintain a perpetual source of attractiveness and interest if selected with a little imagination. And a special word must be said for the whole range of ericas, for here are species, hybrids and varieties

to provide blossom of many forms and colours throughout the year with never a break; many of them offer foliage in several different hues in addition to their flowers.

Several factors come to bear when selecting planting material for stocking a garden with the intention of providing as much colour as possible. One of these is that of size and it is one of the most important. It should be remembered that sharp colour contrasts are rendered more so in confined areas. Sometimes this is acceptable, but may also produce too bright an effect at close quarters; wiser, perhaps, to reduce the number of violent colours in small gardens unless adequate white is used to soften them.

Winter flowering shrubs By judicious planning and selection it should be possible to have shrubs in flower throughout the year. Winter-flowering shrubs make an individual contribution to our gardens, bringing colour and, in many instances, penetrating fragrance during the darkest days of the season.

By mid-November, when the early heavy frosts have stripped the deciduous shrubs and trees of most of their leaves, the first pinkish-white flower clusters of *Viburnum fragrans* will be starting to open. This is one of the loveliest and most useful of winter shrubs; it continues to produce relays of richly fragrant blossoms right up to the end of February. There is a white variety, *candidissima,* with flowers lacking the pinkish tinge of the type, but which contrast even more effectively with the

1 The lilacs, *Syringa vulgaris,* in a variety of colour, are grown for their flower effect
2 The berries of *Clerodendrum fargesii* are of a curious shape
3 Borders can be mixed or confined to plants producing flowers in varying shades of one colour. This mainly yellow border is at its best in early summer when this colour tends to predominate
4 *Cytisus scoparius burkwoodii*

bare, cinnamon-brown twigs.

The witch hazels start to flower towards the end of December and in most seasons it is possible to fill a vase with their curious spidery, cowslip-scented blossoms at Christmas. *Hamamelis mollis,* the Chinese species, with showy golden-yellow flowers —showy by winter standards, at any rate, is the one most widely grown. The form *brevipetala* has shorter petals of orange, while those of *pallida* are a pale sulphur-yellow.

H. japonica comes into flower a little later; the blooms of this species are more striking, their golden-yellow strap-like petals being set off by a purple calyx. They lack, however, much of the scent of the *mollis* varieties.

More fragrant still—half a dozen small sprigs will scent a room—is the winter sweet, *Chimonanthus praecox,* with waxy, pale yellow flowers, the centres blotched with purple. In the variety *grandiflorus*

Red can be a difficult colour to place. Hues and tones are more effective when distributed

White is a key colour which stands on its own merits and acts as an incomparable foil

3

they are of a pure clear yellow. The plant type starts to bloom in December, the flowers of the latter open a few weeks later and sacrifice some of their scent for showiness.

February will see the bare branches of the mezereon, *Daphne mezereum,* covered in purple, hyacinth-scented blossom. This is a short-lived shrub and might well qualify to fill gaps in the border if it did not make such a valuable winter contribution to the garden. Fortunately, fresh supplies come easily from seed, and provided the scarlet fruits—which incidentally are extremely poisonous—are protected from the birds, which are very partial to them, the task of providing replacements is a

4

simple one as the seed will germinate freely in any good garden soil.

From spring to summer the main display starts with shrubs such as the viburnums, brooms and lilacs and reaches its zenith at midsummer.

With the many plants to choose from, planning and planting for continuity of display should be easy. To obtain a lavish display of blossom for as long as possible it will be necessary to include in the planting plan shrubs such as *Caryopteris clandonensis,* and the tree hollyhock, *Hibiscus syriacus,* the flowering season of which covers the months of late summer and autumn.

Lilacs rank among the favourite shrubs of late spring and the most decorative are the hybrids of *Syringa vulgaris.* Among both singles and doubles, old favourites still reign supreme, with 'Souvenir de Louis Spath' as the best purple and 'Maud Notcutt' most popular as the most outstanding single white. Lesser-known single forms include 'Esther Staley', an unusual shade of pale lilac verging on pink, and 'Maurice Barnes', the best examples of the true 'lilac' colour.

Many prefer the doubles with their chunky tightly-packed conical flower trusses, although they lack some of the elegant form of the singles. 'Katherine Havemeyer' (soft mauve), 'Madame Lemoine' (white) are all established favourites. All of them, both single and double have the typical enchanting perfume of lilacs and are vigorous shrubs, reaching a height of 15–20 feet.

In the smaller garden there will not be much room for these giants, but some of the lilac species are much more compact and would prove useful where space is restricted. Their flowers may be smaller and less showy than those of the larger hybrids but they yield nothing to these where fragrance is concerned. *Syringa macrophylla,* for example, makes a dainty shrub, only 4–6 feet in height, with elegant purple flower spikes that are extremely fragrant and have an attractive habit of continuing to bloom at intervals throughout the summer. *S. persica alba,* a white-flowered form of the incorrectly-named 'Persian' lilac is a delightful Chinese shrub with narrow leaves and handsome panicles of white flowers.

In late spring the shrub border is redolent with fine perfumes. The mid-season viburnums, with their distinctive clove scent will be in bloom then; also *V. × burkwoodii,* a vigorous cross between *V. carlesii* and *V. utile,* with its large globes of white, *V. × carlcephalum,* another *carlesii* hybrid, with in this instance, *V. macrocephalum* as the other parent, whose large fragrant flowers measure 4–5 inches across and *V. carlesii* itself, still ranking as one of the most popular garden shrubs.

Midsummer beauty Philadelphus, or mock orange, often wrongly called syringa, will be among the next batch of favourites to come into flower. Its fragrance can be cloying and is too heavy for some tastes. In many of the newer varieties, however, the somewhat funereal smell of *P. coronarius,* is more subdued, and the superb decorative value of their white flowers could never be in dispute. For the smaller gardens of today, there are a number of compact hybrids, much less coarse in habit than the once popular *P. coronarius.* 'Enchantment' is one of the loveliest of these, with elegant, arching branches thickly festooned with double white flowers in June and July. 'Manteau d'Hermine', only 4 feet tall at maturity, also produces its

1

Calcifuges are lime-hating plants such as rhododendrons, camellias and aricas

To fill a garden quickly use some short-lived shrubs as stop-gaps. Alternatively use the more ordinary kinds and remove them when the choicer kinds need more space

1 A border of mixed shrubs selected for either their flower or foliage colour makes a decorative feature
2 Many shrubs are included in the garden for the brilliant colour of their autumn foliage. *Fothergilla monticola* is one of these
3 Rhododendrons are among the most popular of spring flowering shrubs
4 *Garrya elliptica*, excellent in shade

double white blossoms freely. 'Sybille', another delightful shrub of modest dimensions, bears an abundance of dainty white, purple-scented blooms. *P. microphyllus* can be particularly recommended for the small garden. Its leaves are very small and the unusual four-petalled flowers have a distinctive fruity perfume.

Weigelas, still listed sometimes as Diervilla, are useful midsummer shrubs of medium height and girth. Their flowers, borne along the entire length of the previous years' shoots are long and tubular, rather like miniature foxgloves. *W. florida,* a native of Korea and northern China, was discovered by Robert Fortune in the garden of a Chinese mandarin in the last century; it is the hybrids of this attractive species that have produced our popular garden forms.

'Feerie', *W. vanhouttei* and *W. styriaca* are all good, with flowers of varying shades of pink. 'Eva Rathke' and 'Bristol Ruby' have flowers of a stronger colour. 'Eva Rathke' has the longest flowering season. Its deep crimson flowers appear from mid-May until August.

Deutzias, shrubs that deserve wider recognition, will also be in flower at this period. Their habit of growth, narrow at the base but arching elegantly outwards when they attain a height of 4–5 feet,

19

1

2   3

makes them invaluable where ground space is at a premium. The flowers, which are like small tassels, are profusely borne, while in winter the bare cinnamon branches are of great decorative value. *D. elegantissima* is the form most commonly encountered. The pinkish-purple blossoms are profusely borne on arching sprays, while in the variety *pulchra* they are a pearly pink. 'Codsall Pink' is a strong grower and can reach a height of 10–15 feet. This form flowers later than most, starting at the end of June and continuing into July.

No shrub garden would be complete without the summer-flowering viburnums. The snowball bush, *V. opulus sterile,* is the most popular of these. Its globular flowers, green at first, but turning pure white later, make an established specimen of this lovely summer shrub an unforgettable sight when the branches are smothered in white snowballs. It is, however, rather a vigorous grower for small gardens and for these *V. tomentosum plicatum* would be a more appropriate choice. This seldom exceeds 6 or 7 feet in height and the 'snowballs' are in the form of half-globes which are borne in symmetrical pairs along the branches, giving the effect of a stylised Chinese scroll painting. The variety *grandiflorum*, with larger leaves and flowers than those of the type is the best form to grow.

Continuity of display In the rather barren weeks that follow the peak flowering period, hydrangeas are a first-class standby. Apart from the large-leaved species, which require partial shade, they will thrive either in full sun or semi-shade. In the former position, however, copious watering or regular mulching will be required during the first few seasons after planting. *H. macrophylla* is the well-known and deservedly popular pot hydrangea of the florists' shops. It will also do well out of doors in most parts of the British Isles, although in exposed positions and inland districts the blossom buds, which begin to swell very early in the year, may suffer frost damage. This can often be prevented by leaving the previous year's flower-heads on the plants as protection, but in really cold areas it would be safer to plant one of the completely hardy species such as *H. paniculata, H. villosa, H. serrata* or the oak-leaved hydrangea, *H. quercifolia.*

Another genus of late-flowering shrubs, useful for bridging the gap between the summer and the beauties of autumn leaf colour is represented by the hypericums, or St John's worts, of which, the best-known member is the prolific, weed-

1 *Viburnum plicatum tomentosum* Lanarth has its horizontal branches covered in creamy-white flowers in June
2 Red berries of *Vibrunum hupehense*
3 One of the plants grown for its bold red berries is *Skimmia japonica*
4 The feathery foliage of *Rhus typhina laciniata* colours well in autumn
5 The azara species are good shrubs for chalky soil. *Azara lanceolata* has bright yellow double flowers along the arching stems

smothering *H. calycinum*, the rose of Sharon. For the shrub border, however, the taller species and hybrids are a good deal more useful and decorative. Their flowers, like giant buttercups with a central boss of contrasting stamens, make them among the finest shrubs for a late summer display. 'Hidcote' and 'Gold Cup' are both outstanding forms of *H. patulum*, with large cup-shaped flowers 2–2½ inches across. *H. elatum* 'Elstead' is another attractive form, with oval leaves of a fresh vernal green, and masses of small yellow flowers in July and August that are followed by scarlet fruits.

But the outstanding member of the group is undoubtedly the hybrid, 'Rowallane'. Unfortunately, it is not completely hardy in all parts of Britain and needs a sheltered position in many areas. Its magnificent golden chalices are 2½ inches in diameter and well-developed specimens reach a height of 8 feet in milder districts.

To wind up the floral display for the season there is the so-called shrub hollyhock, *Hibiscus syriacus*, together with the blue-flowered *Caryopteris* × *clandonensis*,

which is best treated as a herbaceous perennial and cut back almost to ground level each spring.

Shrubs for autumn leaf colour The beauty of the shrub border is not restricted to its floral display. From September until final leaf fall comes a brilliant cavalcade of coloured foliage, followed by, and sometimes simultaneous with, beauty of winter berry and bark.

Among the shrubs the leaves of which colour so brilliantly, the barberries and cotoneasters play a prominent part. *Berberis thunbergii* has small leaves of a clear green that produce brilliant flame in autumn. The leaves of the variety *atropurpurea*, which are deep purple throughout the summer, assume even more dazzling colours before they fall. *B. verruculosa* is an evergreen species, but many of its dark green leaves turn scarlet, while some of the foliage of the closely related *Mahonia aquifolium*, another evergreen, turns coppery-red in autumn and winter.

Although, botanically, the cut-leaved Japanese maples are not shrubs, but small trees, they have so many of the characteristics of the former that they are usually included in this category.

The Japanese maples are very slow growers and the purple-leaved *Acer palmatum dissectum atropurpureum* and its green-leaved counterpart, *palmatifidum*, both with leaves like the finest lace, never exceed 8–10 feet in height. The leaves of the former turn a vivid deep scarlet, while those of the latter colour to a lighter but no less distinctive hue.

Anyone who gardens on the moist, peaty soils in which rhododendrons and azaleas thrive ought to find room for *Enkianthus campanulatus*, which enjoys similar conditions and puts on a spectacular autumn display in orange and red. The Ghent azaleas, too, can be very colourful in autumn, as also can the common yellow *Azalea pontica* (*Rhododendron ponticum*), when its sage-green leaves burst into tints of flame and coral.

One of the most unusual and striking shrubs for autumn colour, is a member of the euonymus genus, of which the spindle tree is probably the most representative. *E. alata* has leaves that turn a bright glowing pink. After they fall, continuing winter interest is provided by the curious corky wing-like excrescences on the stems.

All the cotinus and rhus, related genera, are noted for their brilliant autumn colour. The stag's horn sumach, *R. typhina laciniata*, is particularly spectacular, but this small tree colours rather early for the main autumn display and the display itself is somewhat short-lived. Much more satisfying are the brilliant orange and scarlets of *Cotinus americanus (Rhus cotinoides)*, or the bright yellow of the smoke bush, *Cotinus coggygria (Rhus cotinus)*.

Among wall shrubs and climbers many of the vines and creepers colour magnificently, particularly the giant-leaved *Vitis coignetiae, Vitis inconstans* (syns. *Parthenocissus tricuspidata veitchii, Ampelopsis veitchii*), and the true Virginian Creeper, *Parthenocissus quinquefolia.* Where space is restricted, the smaller-leaved and less rampant *Parthenocissus henryana* is useful for providing a wall tapestry of brilliant colour.

On the ground, too, creeping and prostrate shrubs such as *Cotoneaster horizontalis, Gaultheria procumbens* and others will be putting down a red carpet, while the hypericums, that have only just finished their flowering season, will be adding to the autumn colours. *Hypericum patulum forrestii* has the most brilliant foliage of any of these.

Beauty of berry and bark Just as decorative, but with a longer-lasting effect are the berries of many shrubs. These will continue the display from leaf fall until the New Year—sometimes even later in districts where birds are not numerous.

Once again, the barberries and cotoneasters are well in evidence, with species and varieties bearing fruits of many colours, ranging from the vivid coral red of *Berberis* 'Bountiful' to the grape-purple of *B. darwinii.* Among the striking forms are *B.* 'Buccaneer' and *B. thunbergii,* both with bright red berries and both, incidentally, also providing attractive leaf colour. 'Cherry Ripe' has fruits that are salmon-red and pear-shaped; the compact, free-flowering Formosan species, *B. morrisonsienis,* bears larger red fruits than most.

More than a dozen kinds of cotoneaster share this same valuable quality. The better known varieties include *C. horizontalis,* whose herring-bone set branches are packed with scarlet button berries and *C. simonsii,* a popular shrub for hedging and cover planting, with no less brilliant berries the size of peas. Taller forms and species include *C. cornubia* with large berries borne profusely, *C. frigidus* with clustered crimson fruits and *C. salicifolius,* the willow-leaved cotoneaster, that bears heavy crops of bright red fruits.

The pernettyas are a group of attractive small-leaved evergreen shrubs with showy marble-sized berries of an unusual beauty. Not many of them, however, are self-fertile so that a specimen of the type plant, *P. mucronata,* will have to be included to cross-fertilise the more decoratively-

berried forms. These last-named include 'Donard Pink' and 'Donard White' (the names are descriptive of the colour of their berries), *lilacina,* with lilac-pink fruits and 'Bell's Seedling' with extra-large, dark-red berries.

The vacciniums, like the pernettyas, are ericaceous plants, and they include the edible North American swamp blueberry,

1

V. corymbosum, and others such as *V. macrocarpum,* the American cranberry, a prostrate evergreen, the large scarlet berries of which are used for cranberry sauce traditionally associated with the Christmas turkey. *V. myrsinites,* the evergreen blueberry, is a graceful compact shrub that bears its blue-black berries in May and June when they are of doubtful value for garden decoration.

Finally, to act as a foil to the winter-flowering shrubs, there are other plants whose main attraction lies in their strikingly-coloured bark or interesting branch formation.

The dogwoods, both the scarlet and yellow-stemmed species, love moisture, while the curiously twisted stems and branches of *Corylus avellana contorta,*

1 The firethorn, *Pyracantha rogersiana,* has red berries
2 The various forms of hibiscus produce flowers in August, a month in which few shrubs flower

2

Certain shrubs are dioecious, with male and female flowers borne on separate plants. A specimen of each sex needs to be planted if there are to be berries

Some of the prostrate forms of cotoneaster make good ground covers. Cotoneaster dammeri and adpressus are examples

make an unusual and interesting tracery against winter skies.

Preparation of the site Just because shrubs *are* so easy to grow, it is a mistake to imagine that you can just stick them into a hole in the ground and then leave them to their own devices. Proper and careful planting is one of the most important operations contributing to their successful cultivation.

The initial preparation of the site should be done, whenever possible, a few months before planting is due to be carried out, in order to give the soil ample opportunity to settle. This may not always be possible, in which case a certain amount of raking and treading may be necessary on light sandy soils, while on heavier clays extra precautions will have to be taken to avoid leaving air pockets round the roots.

Deep and thorough cultivation, either by trenching or double digging, to break up the subsoil, as well as the top spit, is the ideal to be aimed at.

Although the roots of the shrubs will eventually travel far in search of nourishment and moisture, this preliminary cultivation will ensure that they get away to a good start in their first season.

Before the shrubs are put in, the surface soil should be broken down to a reasonably good tilth. Getting it into this condition will provide an opportunity of raking in a slow-acting organic fertiliser, such as steamed bone flour, meat and bonemeal or fish manure. Any of these, applied at the rate of 3–4 ounces per square yard should provide adequate reserves for the first growing season.

With a new garden, on former pasture or woodland, the chances are that the soil will already contain sufficient humus. First, the turf should be sliced off and placed at the bottom of the second spit or, as far as woodland sites are concerned, all fallen leaves, leafmould, etc., should be collected up and incorporated in the soil as digging progresses.

Where existing beds and borders are being given over to shrubs, it may be necessary to provide humus-forming materials in the form of sedge peat, leafmould, garden compost, spent hops, or rotted down straw, when the site is prepared.

Planting holes must be large enough and deep enough to accommodate the roots without bunching or overcrowding, and it is a good idea to leave a slight mound at the base of the hole on which the plant can rest while the roots are spread out and soil is worked among them. On light sandy soils this latter procedure will be simple, but with sticky clays, particularly if planting coincides with a wet spell, it may be necessary to fill in the holes with compost or dry sifted soil. Most shrubs will benefit by being planted in a mixture consisting of equal parts of sifted soil, peat or leafmould and bonfire ash.

Depth of planting is important. The soil mark on the stem made at the nursery can be used as a guide and shrubs should be planted with the soil slightly above this to allow for the slight sinking that is likely to take place.

Normally, staking will not be necessary, although in positions exposed to strong winds it may be advisable to provide a temporary support for the first season to guard against root damage from wind rock. In any case, it is always advisable to go round newly planted shrubs after a spell of rough weather or prolonged frost to refirm the soil round the base.

Shrubs for specific purposes

For partly shaded situations

Acer japonicum (Japanese maple)
Aucuba japonica (spotted laurel)
Berberis (various) (barberry)
Buxus sempervirens (box)
Camellia
Choisya ternata (Mexican orange)
Cotoneaster simonsii
Daphne mezereum (mezereon)
Garrya elliptica (silk tassel bush)
Genista (various) (broom)
Hedera (various) (ivy)
Hypericum (St John's wort)
Ilex (holly)
Kerria japonica (Jew's mallow)
Viburnum tinus (laurustinus)
Mahonia aquifolium (Oregon grape)
Pernettya
Pyracantha (firethorn)
Ruscus aculeatus (butcher's broom)
Sambucus nigra aurea (golden elder)
Vinca major and *Vinca minor* (periwinkle)

Foliage effects

Artemisia abrotanum (southernwood, lad's love)
Arundinaria and Phyllostachys (bamboo)
†*Cornus alba sibirica* and *C. alba variegata* (dogwood)
Cotinus coggygria (smoke bush)
†*Elaeagnus pungens variegata* (wood olive)
Euonymus alata
Hebe (shrubby veronica)

Hypericum patulum (St John's wort)
Laurus nobilis (sweet bay)
Pachysandra terminalis
Phlomis fruticosa (Jerusalem sage)
Ribes americanum (American black currant)
Romneya coulteri (Californian tree poppy)
Rosmarinus officinalis (rosemary)
Ruta graveolens (rue)
Santolina chamaecyparissus (cotton lavender)
Senecio maritima
Sorbaria arborea
Spiraea arguta (bridal wreath)
Viburnum davidii
Vitis coignetiae
†*Weigela florida variegata*
*Good autumn leaf colour
†Variegated foliage

Berried shrubs

Arbutus unedo (strawberry tree)
Aronia arbutifolia (red chokeberry)
Aucuba japonica (spotted laurel)
Berberis (various, barberry)
**Celastrus orbiculata* (climbing bittersweet)
Clerodendrum trichotomum
Gaultheria procumbens (partridge berry)
Hippophaë rhamnoides (sea buckthorn)
Ilex (various, holly)
Pernettya
**Pyracantha* (firethorn)
Skimmia japonica
Symphoricarpos albus laevigatus (snowberry)
Vaccinium myrsinites (evergreen blueberry)

Viburnum (various)
**Wall shrubs

Shrubs for chalk

Aesculus parviflora (bottlebrush buckeye)
Azara microphylla
Berberis (all) (barberry)
Buddleia davidii (butterfly bush)
Choisya ternata (Mexican orange)
Cistus (rock rose)
Cotinus (all)
Cotoneaster (all)
Deutzia
Erica carnea, E. × darleyensis (heaths)
Escallonia (Chilean gum box)
Forsythia (golden bells)
Hibiscus syriacus (tree hollyhock)
Syringa (all) (lilac)
Philadelphus (mock orange)
Potentilla (shrubby cinquefoil)
Rhus (all)
Spiraea (all)
Symphoricarpos (all) (snowberry)
Viburnum (all)

Waterside planting shrubs

Arundinaria, Phyllostachys (bamboo)
Cornus alba, C. stolonifera (dogwood)
Cortaderia (pampas grass)
Philadelphus (mock orange)
Sambucus (elder)
Viburnum opulus sterile (snowball tree)
Weigela

CHAPTER THREE
BEAUTIFUL CLIMBERS

These are the romantics of the garden. Everyone can find a place for at least one climber but the wise gardener will plant many more. House walls, garden walls, fences, archways, pergolas, trellises, poles, either single or erected tripod fashion and other vertical or near-vertical features, provide the gardener with another dimension in which to grow plants. There are attractive plants available for this purpose, many of which benefit from the extra shelter provided by a wall or fence.

Types of plant Suitable plants include those which are true climbers, clinging to some form of support, either by tendrils (e.g. clematis), by twining stems (e.g. honeysuckles) and those known as self-clinging climbers, which adhere to their supports by aerial roots (e.g. the ivies) or by sucker-pads (e.g. the Virginian creeper and some of its relations). In addition to these true climbers, there are many woody or semi-woody plants which are not, in fact, climbers but may be trained against walls. Examples of these are the well-known chaenomeles ('japonica'), climbing roses, ceanothus and certain cotoneasters.

An unusual way of growing certain climbers such as clematis, honeysuckles, is to let them clamber over dead trees or even up the trunks and into the branches of living trees. It is better to avoid for living trees the very vigorous climbers such as *Polygonum baldschuanicum,* the Russian vine, although this is perfectly suitable for a dead tree, which it will quickly smother with its long, twining growths.

Some climbers may easily be grown in well-drained tubs or other large containers and this method is useful where there is no soil bed near the wall, or in courtyards, patios or on town balconies. John Innes potting compost is suitable but vigorous plants may need regular feeding when in

Plastic mesh and plastic trellis are non-rust, non-rot, easily fixed and always attractive

Never treat timber trellis with creosote. It kills plant growth

full growth.

Types of support Self-clinging climbers need little in the way of extra support except in their early stages. Once started they cling to walls, fences and the like and need little more attention. Some gardeners are a little wary of the more vigorous self-clinging climbers such as ivies, but, provided they are not allowed to interfere with drain-pipes, guttering, roof tiles or slates, etc., they are unlikely to harm the wall itself. It can be argued that they help to keep the wall dry and the house warm, by providing a leafy covering which keeps off even the heaviest rain.

Tendril climbers and twining climbers obviously need something to which to cling. In the open, garden poles, driven vertically into the ground or set tripod fashion, pergola posts and archways will provide support for twiners, but not for tendril climbers. These will need further support such as wire-netting placed loosely round the poles to which the tendrils can cling. The growths of non-climbers will need tying in to the support as they develop.

Against walls and fences there are various ways of providing support for plants. Trellis-work is a well-tried method and panels may be bought in various sizes.

Panels of plastic-covered, heavy gauge wire-netting (Gro-Mesh) are obtainable in various sizes, and these provide excellent support for plants. They may be fixed to the wall in much the same way as wooden trellis.

Wires, preferably covered, stretched across the face of a wall or fence, about an inch away from it, will also provide adequate support for many plants. However, unless the wire is properly strained it may sag in course of time. Vine eyes (drive-in pattern for walls, driven into the perpendicular jointing, screw-in type for wooden posts) are useful devices for fixing wires for climbing plants. Straining bolts, which can be tightened when necessary to take up any slack, are also obtainable. Lead-headed wall nails, nails with flexible lead tags, are used for individual ties, when it becomes necessary to tie in long, woody growths such as those of climbing

1 *Cobaea scandens,* a half-hardy climbing plant from South America
2 *Passiflora caerulea,* a beautiful climber for warm walls
3 *Thunbergia alata,* Black-eyed Susan, an annual
4 Morning Glory or Ipomoea (a synonym for *Pharbitis tricolor*), an annual climber

or rambler roses.

Flowering climbers on a house are so enchanting. The sweetly scented wisteria is a great favourite.

Cultivation Wisterias will grow in any ordinary well-drained soil. A sunny, sheltered position is essential. Provide adequate support for displaying the hanging 'chains' to best advantage. Unnecessary vigorous shoots should be cut hard back in winter. Flowering takes place on short spur growths which should be encouraged.

I grow one of the lovely solanums on a west wall. There are others, really tall shrubs rather than climbers. Nearby I grow clematis.

Clematis (klem-a-tis or klem-ay-tis)
Clematis comprise the most useful and diverse group of shrubby climbing plants. The name is derived from the Greek *klema*, a vine branch, referring to their climbing habit. The large-flowered cultivars are showy and glamorous, and the smaller flowered species and hybrids are singularly adaptable and vigorous, and carry quantities of blossom. A wide selection of clematis may be had in flower from April until October.

All of them need some sort of support, unless they are being used as ground coverers. On a wall, they will cling to lattice, wires or to other wall shrubs such as wisteria, pyracantha or roses. Most clematis will flower as freely on a north aspect as elsewhere. Perhaps they look their best when growing in the open over other shrubs, such as lilacs, viburnums and shrub roses. Or they can be trained, with the help of some wire-netting, over tree stumps or used among heather to extend the heath garden's season of interest. They also make an effective vertical feature on a pole, arising from among lower shrubs or herbaceous plants.

Clematis in cultivation Most clematis

2

1

3

Always keep clematis roots in the shade and flowers in the sun

Make sure your climber supports are strong and spreading before you plant; it will be too late when the plant is growing vigorously

are deciduous and very hardy. The few worthwhile evergreen species need a sheltered wall for protection.

Pruning Methods of pruning of climbing clematis vary according to the season of flowering. They can be considered under three headings. (1) Early spring flowering. These include the small-flowered species *C. alpina*, *C. macropetala*, *C. armandii*, *C. montana*, *C. chrysocoma*, *C. spooneri* and all their varieties and cultivars. They need no regular pruning but if they become leggy or out of hand or are required to occupy only a small space, they can have all their flowering trails removed *immediately after flowering*.

(2) Early summer flowering, large-flowered cultivars, both single and double, that have already been considered as a group. It is perfectly natural for a good deal of flowering wood, in these, to die at the end of the growing season. All dead shoots should be removed in February or March when new growth is sufficiently advanced for live and dead to be easily distinguished. Thus, pruning consists in thinning out. (3) The species and large-flowered cultivars with a flowering season from late June onwards should be cut hard back, annually, to within a foot or two of ground level. The safest time is March, but the plants look so unsightly in winter that many gardeners take a chance on pruning them in November, which is usually safe enough in our British climate.

If you want your climbers to do really well and reward you handsomely, then you must ensure that they are planted properly. The site should be well dug and adequately drained where necessary.

Planting The footings of walls usually

1 *Clematis montana rubens* given an Award of Merit in 1905
2 *Wisteria sinensis,* a favourite climbing plant, flowers in May
3 One of several forms of *Wisteria floribunda,* with long racemes of purple and white flowers
4 A tall shrub which is almost a climber, *Solanum crispum autumnale,* has showy purplish-blue flowers
5 *Clematis patens* 'Nellie Moser', deservedly very popular, flowers profusely in early summer
6 *Clematis florida sieboldii,* a synonym for Clematis bicolor, a striking and rare form, given an Award of Merit in 1914. The central boss is composed of purple, petal-like stamens

4

5   6

project several inches beyond the line of the wall itself and to avoid these and the drier soil at the base of the wall, the plant should not be closer to the foot of the wall than 6 inches. Where there is enough room, a planting hole about 2 feet wide and $1\frac{1}{2}$–2 feet deep should be taken out, to allow sufficient room for the roots to be spread out properly. If the soil is heavy clay it is better not to replace it but to use instead some specially made up planting soil. The basis of this might be old potting soil or good loam to which should be added generous quantities of garden compost and leafmould plus a couple of handfuls of bonemeal per barrow-load of the mixture to provide slow-acting food.

Some temporary support should be provided for the plants until their growths reach the wire, trellis or other support and can begin to cling or twine. Even though this is temporary it should be firmly fixed to prevent the growths blowing about and being damaged. Short canes, twiggy sticks, strings or wires fixed to pegs driven into the ground, are all suitable.

Training and pruning Left to their own devices many climbers quickly become a tangled mass of growths, new shoots clinging to or twining round older ones, instead of neatly covering the supports provided and filling their allotted spaces. Some initial training may be needed to overcome this tendency. Such training consists in starting the new shoots off in the right direction and occasionally during the season ensuring that they are carrying on in the way they are desired to go. This is particularly necessary where it is required to train the shoots horizontally or nearly horizontally, since the natural growth of the plant is upward.

Shrubs trained flat against walls and fences usually need to have their breast-wood removed from time to time. Very young growths developing from forward-pointing buds can often be rubbed out to prevent their development; otherwise the secateurs will have to be used judiciously.

Pruning is often needed to keep plants under control or to ensure the production of new flowering growths.

Mulching An annual mulch round the bases of the plants, but not actually touching the stems, will help to prevent the soil from drying out in hot weather, particularly near walls and fences, will keep down weeds and will supply plant foods and improve the soil texture as the mulch is gradually absorbed into the soil by the action of worms and weather. Such a mulch might consist of garden compost, leafmould, partially rotted leaves, or moist peat. Late spring is a suitable time to

apply the mulch which should be several inches deep. The covering may be renewed from time to time during the summer.

Providing protection Some slightly tender plants may be grown successfully against walls in many parts of the country although in severe weather some protection may be necessary.

1 *Clematis macropetala,* a Chinese species that obtained the Award of Merit in 1923 and Award of Garden Merit in 1934
2 Hedera 'Jubilee', a distinctive ivy with elegantly pointed variegated leaves
3 *C. jackmanii superba*
4 *Clematis jackmanii* 'Comtesse de Bouchaud' given an Award of Merit in 1936
5 The climbing form of the rose 'Caroline Testout' is ideal for a pergola. Flowering is almost continuous from June to November

1

3

2

Climbers for Particular Purposes

Annual

Cobaea (P as A)	Maurandya	Rhodochiton
Cucurbita	(P as A)	(P as A)
Humulus (P as A)	Mina	Thunbergia
Ipomoea	Pharbitis	Tropaeolum
Lathyrus		

Greenhouse

Allamanda	Dolichos	Pentapterygium
Antigonon	Eccremocarpus	Petraea
Araujia	Ficus	Philodendron
Aristolochia	Gloriosa	Piper
Asparagus	Hedera	Plumbago
Bomarea	Hibbertia	Rhodochiton
Bauhinia	Hoya	Rhoicissus
Beaumontia	Ipomoea	Smilax
Bougainvillea	Jasminum	Solanum
Cassia	Lapageria	Sollya
Cestrum	Metrosideros	Stephanotis
Cissus	Mikania	Streptosolen
Clerodendrum	Mitraria	Syngonium
Clianthus	Monstera	Thunbergia
Cobaea	Myrsiphyllum	Tibouchina
Colquhounia	Oxypetalum	Trachelosper-
Convolvulus	Parthenocissus	mum
Dipladenia	Passiflora	Tropaeolum

Tendril

Ampelopsis (D)	Lathyrus (D)	Passiflora (E)
Clematis (D & E)	Mutisia (E)	Smilax (D & E)
Eccremocarpus	Parthenocissus	Vitis (D)
(D)	(D)	

Twining

Actinidia (D)	Jasminum	Pueraria (D)
Akebia (SE)	(D & E)	Schizandra (D)
Araujia (E)	Kadsura (E)	Senecio (D)
Aristolochia (D)	Lardizabala (E)	Solanum (D)
Berberidopsis (E)	Lonicera (D & E)	Sollya (E)
Billardiera (E)	Mandevilla (D)	Stauntonia (E)
Calystegia (D)	Muehlenbeckia	Trachelospermum
Celastrus (D)	(D)	(E)
Holboellia (E)	Periploca (D)	Wistaria (D)
Humulus (D)	Polygonum (D)	

Walls north and east

Berberidopsis	Hydrangea	Pileostegia (E)
(E)	(D & E)	Vitis (D)
Ficus (E)	Jasminum (D & E)	
Hedera (E)	Lonicera (D & E)	

Shrubs, Wall plants (not true climbers)

Abelia (D & E)	Cotoneaster	Indigofera (D)
Abutilon (D)	(D & E)	Itea (D & E)
Adenocarpus	Diplacus (D)	Jasminum (D & E)
(D or SE)	Escallonia	Kerria (D)
Buddleia (D & E)	(D & E)	Magnolia (D & E)
Camellia (E)	Feijoa (E)	Phygelius (E)
Ceanothus (D & E)	Forsythia (D)	Piptanthus (E)
Ceratostigma (D)	Fremontia (D)	Pyracantha (E)
Chaenomeles (D)	Garrya (E)	Ribes (D)
Colletia (D)	Hebe (E)	Rosa (D & E)
Corokia (E)	Hypericum	Rubus (D)
Crinodendron (E)	(D & E)	Schizandra (D)

Note: For full details of the genera listed in these tables reference should be made to the specific articles in this Encyclopedia.

Key: D Deciduous. E Evergreen. P as A Perennial grown as annual. SE Semi-evergreen.

Rambling and climbing roses

Good ramblers mainly descended from *R. multiflora* and *R. luciae*, variety *wichuraiana*

Name	Colour
Crimson Shower	Crimson
Débutante	Pink
Excelsa	Scarlet crimson
Félicité et Perpetué	Milk white
Francis E. Lester	Blush, single
Goldfinch	Pale yellow
Sanders' White	White
Violette	Purple

Large-flowered ramblers mainly derived from *R. luciae*

Albéric Barbier	Creamy yellow
Albertine	Coppery pink
Breeze Hill	Straw yellow
Emily Gray	Yellow
François Juranville	Salmon pink
Mary Wallace	Pink
May Queen	Lilac pink
Paul Transon	Coppery pink

Climbers of hybrid tea style

Climbing Etoile de Hollande	Dark crimson
Climbing Mme Butterfly	Light pink
Climbing Mme Caroline Testout	Pink
Climbing McGredy's Ivory	White
Climbing Mrs Sam McGredy	Coppery red
Easlea's Golden Rambler	Yellow
Guinée	Maroon
Mme Grégoire Staechelin	Deep pink
Paul's Lemon Pillar	Lemon white

Floribunda climbers

Climbing Allgold	Yellow
Coral Dawn	Coral pink
Danse du Feu	Orange red
Dream Girl	Coppery salmon
Kassel	Coppery red
Leverkusen	Pale yellow
Nymphenburg	Salmon pink
Parade	Crimson pink
Pink Cloud	Clear pink

CHAPTER FOUR
PEAT FOR VARIETY

The easiest way to keep plants happy is to plant them in a soil which suits them. Some soils are just plain ordinary and there are hundreds of plants that will grow happily in them so long as they have proper nourishment. Others have a high lime content or may be acid. There are plants for both extremes. You can make a limy soil more neutral by using peat as a deep annual mulch or by incorporating plenty of it into the topsoil.

Lime-hating plants
Plants which dislike lime are those which will not grow in any soil which has a *p*H value (the scale for measuring the acidity or alkalinity of the soil) of more than 7·0. The reasons for this are complex, but briefly, in such a soil some mineral nutrients become less available to the plant roots, for example iron, magnesium or manganese. Consequently the plant suffers from one or more nutrient deficiencies: if iron is lacking, the tip leaves become pale, almost white, manganese deficiency shows as yellowing between the leaf veins, and so on. With some plants the trouble is even more marked in that the roots never develop at all and the plant simply dies very soon after planting.

It is not easy to grow lime-hating plants in alkaline soils, and they may never do as well as they would in acid soils, but it can be done.

There are one or two chemicals which can be added to the soil to help the plants take up the right nutrients.

The group of chemicals known as sequestrols have been specially formulated to overcome the difficulty. Iron, magnesium, manganese and so on are present in these substances in such a form that, when mixed with water and added to the soil, they can easily be absorbed by the plant roots—thus the plant no longer suffers from a deficiency. They do not make an alkaline soil into an acid one.

Lime-hating plants include the family *Ericaceae*, for instance most rhododendrons, azaleas and heathers (except *Erica carnea*). Others are camellias, *Cornus kousa* and *C. sinensis*, halesias, liquidambars, some magnolias and styrax. Herbaceous plants and alpines, on the whole, are tolerant of lime, although lupins and *Lithospermum prostratum* grow badly, if at all, in alkaline soils.

Peat beds
It has been discovered that walls composed of peat blocks can be built up from the ground level to enclose an area which, when filled with acid peaty soil, will provide suitable situations for a number of plants which need just such soil conditions. If the normal soil of the garden is an alkaline one this allows you to grow many fine plants, especially among the *Ericaceae*, *Primulaceae* and *Pinaceae*, which you may otherwise have to forego.

A semi-shady site is most suitable, such as below a tree or on the north side of a

1 A path runs between borders richly planted with shrubs and perennials at Branklyn, near Perth
2 Rhododendrons and brooms flourish to perfection at Inverewe, Wester Ross
3 Hydrangeas will normally produce blue flowers only on acid soils
4 *Enkianthus campanulatus,* a shrub growing to 8 feet that requires lime-free soil. Light shade is tolerated
5 A number of plants will not grow properly, if at all, in limy soils. Such plants include camellias

It is always wise to test the soil in your garden. Simple kits are available from garden stores and most chemists

During the autumn months the whorls of the enkianthus leaves are beautifully coloured

hedge or fence. If the soil is neutral fork it over first; if it is alkaline it is best to leave it but to lay down a 3–4 inch thick layer of rough peat before starting to build the wall.

I have several raised peat beds on my own limy soil and here I grow the lovely plants such as rhododendrons, azaleas and ericas that would otherwise be denied me.

Some of the most agreeable of the peat loving plants are the heathers.

The majority are compact, dwarf-growing, but some species attain the height of small trees. Most species require a lime-free soil, although *E. carnea* and its varieties, *E. × Darleyensis, E. mediterranea, E. terminalis* and the tree heath, *E. arborea*, are to a varying degree tolerant of chalky soil. Hardy heaths are most effective and thrive better when grouped together than when dotted about singly. They are excellent plants for suppressing weeds. By making a careful selection it is possible to have heathers in flower in the garden almost throughout the year, provided there is sufficient space for a comprehensive collection.

I was once lucky enough to see kalmia growing wild in America and I have loved it ever since. These are evergreen and, rarely, deciduous shrubs with dark, glossy leaves and exquisitely shaped waxy flowers. They thrive in an acid soil in dappled shade.

There just isn't space to describe all the fabulous rhododendrons there are.

Rhododendron (ro-do-den-dron)

This is a large genus, with up to 600 species, ranging from prostrate alpine plants to tree-like specimens, some with enormous leaves. It includes those plants which were at one time described under the genus *Azalea* and others which were once included in the genus *Rhodora*. There are both evergreen and deciduous species and hybrids. One point which they have in common is that they will not tolerate lime in the soil, except for those mentioned below. The greatest number of species has been introduced from western China, Tibet, north-western India and Burma; there are also a few from Java and Malaysia, which require warm greenhouse conditions when grown in the British Isles. As there are probably well over 200 species and many hundreds of hybrids in cultivation, it is possible here to describe a selection only, under the main headings.

These are: *rhododendron section* species cultivated: hardy; tender; hybrids, hardy; *azalea section* species cultivated: hybrids, deciduous, mollis, Ghent, occidentalis,

double mollis, double Ghent, Knap Hill and Exbury hybrids, evergreen hybrids. Those readers who require further details of species and hybrids in cultivation should refer to specialist works on the genus *Rhododendron* and to the catalogues of nurserymen who specialise in the genus.

Azalea section The first essential for azaleas is a lime-free soil and they grow best in a sandy loam containing plenty of leaf soil or peat, even a trace of clay, but they dislike a heavy wet soil or being baked dry at the roots in summer. They will flower well in full sun, provided that the roots remain reasonably moist and cool, and when grown in an open sunny position the colours are often more intense and the attractive bronze tint to the young leaves in spring is more pronounced, whereas in partial shade this may be absent. Nevertheless azaleas are admirable for a woodland garden in dappled shade and the trees not only provide a beautiful setting, but afford some protection to the blooms which may otherwise be damaged

1 The tubular flowers of *Rhododendron keysii*
2 *Erica vulgaris* makes a low hedge
3 *Kalmia latifolia* 'Brilliant' has full heads of deep pink flowers
4 *Kalmia latifolia,* the Calico Bush is an evergreen with waxy pink flowers
5 Exbury hybrid azaleas, such as this apricot seedling, have been evolved at the Exbury estate, Hampshire, over a large number of years

by late spring frosts.

Azaleas associate well with maples (*acers*), hardy heathers, kalmias, enkianthus and small-growing shrubs in the rhododendron section of the genus, all of which thrive in an acid or lime-free, well-drained soil. The maximum effect is obtained by planting in groups, even of three, if space does not permit for more liberal planting. As they can be lifted with a good ball of soil attached to the roots, planting may be done at any time during the dormant season from late October to about mid-March. Well-budded young plants will usually flower quite happily the first season after being planted. A mulch each autumn of leaf soil, moist peat, or garden compost will keep the shrubs in good condition and farmyard manure, spread at any time from autumn to early spring around the plants, makes a first-class feed, far better than quick-acting fertilisers, which should be avoided. Poultry manure should not be used. Wood ash contains a high proportion of lime, and this should be used sparingly, if at all.

Deciduous hybrids azaleas

Hardy, hybrid azaleas are unsurpassed for brilliance and diversity of colour in the spring and early summer. Autumn colour of foliage is often splendid.

Mollis hybrids These grow 4–5 feet tall, and bear large trusses of scentless flowers, of almost translucent texture, which start to open in early May, before the leaves unfold.

Ghent hybrids These reach 6–8 feet tall and have elegant, tubular, honeysuckle shaped fragrant flowers, which open in late May and early June when the leaves have developed.

Double Mollis and double Ghent hybrids These are 5–8 feet tall, with fragrant flowers in late May and June. Cultivars include 'Aida', rose-pink with deeper flush; 'Byron', white, tinged rose; 'Norma', bright rose; 'Phidias', cream, flushed rose.

Azalea occidentalis hybrids *(R. occidentale)* Plants in this group grow up to 10 feet tall, and have large trusses of fragrant flowers from mid-May to early June, in delicate shades of pink, cream or white flushed with pink.

Knap Hill hybrids and Exbury hybrids These grow 4–8 feet tall. They are two

splendid strains which have been evolved over the years at the Knap Hill Nursery near Woking, Surrey, and at the Rothschild's estate at Exbury, near Southampton. Leading nurserymen offer numerous named varieties as well as plants raised from seed collected from selected, outstanding plants. The flowers are in shades of apricot, flame, pink, crimson, orange, yellow and cream, from early May to mid-June. Double-flowered varieties are also now available.

Evergreen hybrid azaleas

The heights of these range from 2–6 feet. They were mainly raised by plant breeders in Japan and in Europe. Some start to flower in April but the majority are at their best in May when they are profusely covered with bloom.

Hardy hybrids These hybrids range from those of dwarf and medium habit, suitable for a small garden, to those which eventually develop into large shrubs or trees suitable for a spacious woodland setting. The diversity of colour and form of the individual flowers are remarkable.

When you make a peat wall it should be battered, i.e., sloped slightly backwards

Although peat is acid it is unlikely to make other soils appreciably more acid unless very large amounts are used regularly or a very acid peat is used

The hardy hybrid rhododenrons range from small shrubs to near trees in height
1 Rhododendron 'Mermaid'
2 Rhododendron 'Queen Wilhelmina'
3 Rhododendron 'Susan' has mauve flowers
4 *Rhododendron quinquefolium,* from Japan, has broad, ball-shaped white flowers and deciduous pale green leaves
5 The lily-of-the-valley like flowers of *Arbutus unedo,* the Strawberry Tree
6 *Camellia sasanqua* is a winter-flowering Chinese species
7 'Donation'
8 Azaleas (the same genus as rhododendron), as well as most other members of the heather or erica family, dislike limy soils

Camellia

The value of the camellia as an outdoor evergreen flowering shrub, is not always fully appreciated; for long treated as tender, it is now taking its place with rhododendrons and azaleas among hardy shrubs. The leaves are dark glossy green, the flowers white, pink, or red, sometimes attractively striped, mostly borne in March and April (earlier under glass). Height varies according to conditions and can be 15 feet or more. Plants have the advantage of flowering when very young, at only 1½ feet. These shrubs require a position sheltered from cold winds and early morning sun; it is the latter, causing a quick thaw which damages the blooms on frosty mornings. Light woodland or north-facing borders should be chosen.

GARDENING ON CLAY

Clay soils and their improvements

Gardening on clay can be a frustrating and disappointing business unless you are prepared to work hard to cultivate the soil before you attempt to plant it. Most clay soils are difficult to work but when properly managed are fertile and capable of supporting strong growth of a wide range of plants. Their nature varies according to the proportion of pure clay contained in them and when the amount is high the soil is badly drained, sticky and heavy with the large quantities of water they hold. The high content of water also delays their warming up in spring and because of this, early sowing and planting cannot begin until the season is well advanced. Draining is therefore a vital first step towards the improvement of some of these soils. While some may need elaborate drainage systems to bring about success, others may improve with systematic cultivation over a few years.

Virgin land with a high proportion of clay should be double dug when turning it over the first time. This is necessary to break up the hard layer of compacted soil a spade's depth down which so often prevents water escaping from the surface. Digging should be done in autumn and the top soil left in large lumps as deposited from the spade in order that alternate frosts and rain may help to break it down into small crumbs ready for the preparation of seed beds in spring.

Small chippings can be mixed into the soil at the bottom of the trench formed while double digging is being done and will help to keep the soil open. Manures, peat, weathered ashes and crushed clinker give similar benefit. Stones already in the soil should be left in as they will assist drainage.

Horse manure is the best kind to use on clay soils. This is because it is light, drier and less sticky than other animal manures. Near towns, horse manure is often obtainable from riding stables, but in districts where it cannot easily be obtained, com-

1 Philadelphus, mock orange, often erroneously called Syringa, will grow in clay soil. This is the double fragrant, 'Virginal'
2 Viola 'Maggie Mott' requiring good drainage
3 *Crinum x powellii,* for a south-facing well-drained border
4 *Eremurus elwesii alba* flowers in May on stems 6 to 9 feet in height. A warm sunny position is advisable: clay soil is tolerated with an annual mulch

post may be used instead or the land may be seeded with quick growing crops such as mustard, rape, agricultural lupins or vetches which can be dug in as green manure before the flowering stage is reached.

Ridging may be necessary if the soil is very heavy and almost impossible to break down in spring. This method exposes a larger surface of soil to the action of the weather and to be fully effective it must be started in the autumn and the ground left rough throughout the winter. In spring, the soil should be levelled out and forked but no deeper than 4–6 inches, otherwise wet soil from below is brought up to the surface and the purpose of the operation is spoiled. Substantial amounts of coarse sand, grit or horticultural grade peat may be worked in at the same time to improve the surface soil.

Lime is a valuable conditioner to use for improving the physical structure of all clay soils. It binds the small particles together into small crumbs allowing water to pass into the sub-soil and air to dry out the top soil. It helps to convert soil chemicals into plant food, and accelerates the decomposition of organic material which is often slow rotting in clay. It also neutralises acids which are often excessive and the cause of disease in this kind of soil.

Apply the lime after digging is finished. Quick lime is a valuable form to use on the heaviest clays and should be applied in heaps ready for spreading out at rates of 6–12 oz per square yard. Hydrated lime is more pleasant to use and should be spread out evenly over the ground at rates of 8–16 oz per square yard. Lime should not be used within a month of manuring and after application should be left on the soil surface to be washed in by rain.

Manufactured soil conditioners are now used extensively for improving all kinds of soils. These are often based on sodium alginate, a substance obtained from seaweed. The effect on clay soils is to bind or flocculate numerous tiny particles, forming a crumb structure to aid drainage and aeration. A soil conditioner may be used at any time of the year but on vacant land the maximum benefit is obtained by applying it a few days before sowing or planting in the spring. In the growing season it may be sprinkled on the ground between rows or around plants and worked in with a hoe or rake. It may also be applied to lawns after spiking in spring or autumn.

Certain fertilisers cause a marked deterioration in the structure and chemical state of clay soils. Superphosphate of lime makes the soil acid and basic slag applied in late autumn or winter should be used

instead. Sulphate of ammonia is another fertiliser which has the same effect, while nitrate of soda can make the soil sticky and ruin its crumb structure by deflocculating the clay particles. Both sulphate of ammonia and nitrate of soda can be replaced by Nitro-chalk which is applied either as a base dressing before planting or for topdressing around plants in growth.

A way of improving clay soils, used less often nowadays but still very well worthwhile, is to burn it. The method consists in building a wood fire large enough to keep up a good heat for a time and enclose it with large clods of clay so that practically all air is excluded. The clay should not be

1 *Crataegus x lavallei,* a synonym of *C. x carrierei,* a tree that can reach 20 feet. It is a hybrid raised about 1870 at the Jardin des Plantes, Paris
2 The attractive *C. oxyacantha paulii,* a double form
3 Kniphofia 'springtime', typical of the Red Hot Pokers.
4 The tangerine coloured flowers of *Buddleia globosa,* familiarly known as the Orange-ball Tree
5 *Buddleia davidii* is the most popular kind, known as the Butterfly Bush because its spikes of bloom in the late summer attract these insects
6 A modern aquilegia hybrid. Much of their beauty comes from the long spurs behind the flowers

severely burnt; it is sufficient to burn it so that the lumps crumble readily. Clay burned in this way will not return to its previous form but when added to the soil lightens it, enables moisture to penetrate more readily, improves the condition generally and makes potash available. It may not be practicable to deal with large areas in this way but it is worth tackling a small area each year.

During hot weather in spring and summer large cracks appear in clay as it dries out and shrinks. Very often these cracks form along rows of small seedlings, probably because the amount of water taken up by them causes more rapid shrinkage of the soil in that area. To avoid this, the soil must be hoed regularly to keep the surface loose and prevent evaporation of water from just beneath the surface. Mulching with manure, compost, lawn mowings or black polythene will serve the same purpose.

Finally, keep off the soil if it is very wet.

In spring, try to start work on preparing seedbeds just before the soil dries out completely. Some clay soils become brick hard and almost impossible to break up when dry.

What peat does Like all humus suppliers it makes soils more porous by giving them a kind of Aertex structure by virtue of the millions of small cells that make up its fibrous structure. As a result heavy soils are opened up and light soils hold more moisture for plant use. Peat is scattered in drills for vegetable crops, the seedlings are able to push their way through the more difficult soils, which form hard crusts during dry periods.

One of the reasons for the popularity of peat is the ease with which it is spread and mixed with the soil; it is also weed free, clean to handle and has a long-lasting effect on the soil.

But always thoroughly moisten the peat first; never work it in dry otherwise it will stay dry and fail to give the best results. If

6

5

peat is to be used in quantity one way of ensuring that it is properly moistened is to break up the bale, and either allow it to be soaked by rain or apply water with a hose and sprinkler, which may take quite a time. Another way is to make a hole in the bale and insert the hose nozzle and allow water to trickle in gently until the bale is thoroughly soaked through. Even then it may be necessary to break up the bale afterwards and use the sprinkler to make sure that there are no dry patches left.

Smaller quantities can be moistened by soaking over-night in a bucket or other container, after breaking up the lumps by hand. The next day the excess water should be squeezed out before the peat is used.

For overcoming the harmful effects of crusting, scatter 3 ounces of peat per square yard run when preparing seed drills. To help the roots of trees and shrubs to spread evenly through poorly structured soils, put 2 or 3 lb of peat in under each plant when planting shrubs, roses or fruit bushes; a handful is all that is needed for herbaceous plants. Always mix peat with a little loose soil before positioning the plant.

Mulches of peat help to keep shrub and flower borders free from weeds and the soil moist during the summer after which the material can be worked into the soil. A $\frac{1}{16}$ to $\frac{1}{2}$ inch grade product, when applied at the rate of 6–10 lb per square yard, is best for this work.

When preparing the soil for sowing lawn seed or laying turves, peat worked into the top 2 inches, will give a good start to the germinating seeds or help the turves to knit together. A special grade peat is supplied for autumn dressing of lawns.

Peat pots are being increasingly used for seedlings and bedding plants. The pot is put into the soil thus leaving the roots undisturbed. The roots penetrate the peat and finally it is broken down into the soil.

1

2

3

4

Cover bare soil with a deep layer of grass cuttings. As these decompose they will add humus to the soil

Good mulches of peat around the roses will save hoeing and possibly injuring the surface roots

1 *Campanula portenschlagiana,* a hardy trailing June flowering plant
2 *Cotoneaster Conspicuus,* a wide-spreading shrub reaching 4 to 5 feet in height. An Award of Merit was given in 1933
3 *Rosa damascena versicolor,* the 'York and Lancaster' rose, was known prior to 1629. The flowers are pink or white or parti-coloured but not striped as in *Rosa gallica versicolor* ('Rosa mundi')
4 *Rosa gallica versicolor.* 'Rosa mundi', has grown since the sixteenth century, when it was first recorded
5 Hostas, plantain lilies, flourishing at Benmore
6 The berries of *Viburnun lantana* are first red, ripening to black
7 The ribbed leaves and deep blue berries of *Viburnum davidii*
8 *Viburnum opulus fructo-luteo,* the yellow-fruited form of the Guelder Rose, or Snowball Tree

Some Plants Suitable for Clay Soils

Achillea (HP)	Deutzia (S)	Jasminum (S)	Ribes (S)
Aconitum (HP)	Diervilla (S)	Juniperus (T)	Rudbeckia (HP)
Althaea (HP)	Digitalis (HBi/P)	Kerria (S)	Rhus (S)
Anchusa (HP)	Doronicum (HP)	Kniphofia (HP)	Robinia (S/T)
Anemone (HP)	Echinops (HP)	Laburnum (T)	Salix (T)
Aquilegia (HP)	Ericas (S)	Laurus (S/T)	Senecio (HP/S)
Aster (HP)	Escallonia (S)	Lonicera (S)	Skimmia (S)
Berberis (S)	Euonymus (S)	Lupinus (HP)	Solidago (HP)
Bergenia (HP)	Forsythia (S)	Lythrum (HP)	Sorbus (T)
Betula (T)	Galega (HP)	Mehonia (S)	Spiraea (S)
Buddleia (S)	Geranium (HP/RP)	Narcissus (Bu)	Symphoricarpos (S)
Buxus (S)	Geum (HP)	Nepeta (HP)	Syringa (S)
Campanula (HP/RP)	Hebe (S)	Papaver (HP)	Taxus (T)
Cercis (T)	Helenium (HP)	Philadelphus (S)	Thuya (T)
Chaenomeles (S)	Helianthus (HP)	Picea (T)	Tradescantia (HP)
Chamaecyparis (T)	Heliopsis (HP)	Potentilla (HP/S)	Trollius (HP)
Chrysanthemum (HP)	Helleborus (HP)	Primula (HP/RP)	Verbascum (HBi/P)
Cotinus (S)	Hemerocallis (HP)	Prunus (S)	Veronica (HP)
Cotoneaster (S)	Hydrangea (S)	Pyracantha (S)	Viburnum (S/T)
Crataegus (S/T)	Ilex (S/T)	Quercus (T)	Vinca (S)
Daphne (S)	Iris (HP)	Rosa (S)	Viola (HP)

Bi Biennial, Bu Bulb, H Herbaceous, P Perennial, RP Rock Plant, S Shrub, T Tree

Note: The great majority of plants, including vegetables and fruit, will grow successfully on clay soils; those listed above are merely a few of those which do exceptionally well.

CHAPTER SIX
GARDENING ON CHALK

1

Chalky soils

So much is heard about the beauties of the rhododendrons, azaleas, pieris, summer-flowering heaths, embothriums, stewartias and some of the magnolias that the gardener whose land is on chalk or limestone is left feeling rather deprived. There is, however, no need for disappointment. There are quite as many lovely, colourful, free-flowering and fruiting plants which will thrive in alkaline conditions as on acid soils and, provided that the gardener on chalk or lime is prepared to go to the trouble to understand her soil and to meet its problems she will get just as good results from her garden as the woman who gardens on any other type of land.

Two main types of alkaline soils are to be found in Britain—the shallow, hungry soil overlying chalk or limestone rock and the heavy, sticky limy clay known as marl. In addition to these two naturally occurring alkaline soils one sometimes finds old vegetable gardens and similar sites

1 One of the small enclosed gardens at Northbourne Court, Kent
2 *Geranium atlanticum* 9 inches, flowers in summer
3 *Scabiosa caucasica* 'Sarah Cramphorn'
4 *Sempervivum,* the familiar houseleek
5 The Oriental poppy, *Papaver orientale,* of which there are many forms
6 *Agapanthus campanulatus,* the African Lily, flourishes at the base of a sunny wall in well-drained soil
7 Carnations are among the many plants that flourish on chalky soils

which have a high alkalinity due to years of over-liming by their owners. These are best corrected by refraining from adding further lime and, instead, digging in quantities of acid material such as rotted

2

The types of vegetation found growing on calcareous soils often differ tremendously and depend upon the depth of soil on top of the chalk

Some of the most easily worked soil is in areas where the chalk is some 2-3 feet below the surface. It retains moisture and yet any excess is quickly drained

3

4

6

7

5

bracken, poultry manure composted with baled straw built up in layers (4 inches of straw to 2 inches of manure) and allowed to stand for a year before use. An acid grade of peat, garden refuse composted with a non-alkaline activator such as *Fertosan* or *Alginure* and litter from deep-litter poultry are also valuable. Where water-logging occurs however, a drainage system is necessary and this should be provided before any attempt is made to treat the soil.

Light alkaline soils overlying chalk and limestone are 'hungry', absorbing all added nutriment almost as quickly as it is added, thus being just as poor as before. On such soils it is necessary to add organic matter at every opportunity—the coarser the better so as to slow down the process of decomposition. Animal manure, poultry manure composted with straw, spent hops, hop-manure, peat, seaweed and leafmould from acid-soil areas all help. In addition every possible scrap of vegetable and animal waste should be composted ready to be dug into the soil or added as a surface mulch.

Another difficulty to be encountered on these shallow alkaline soils is the lack of depth and consequent drying out. This can be counteracted by excavating good individual holes for all permanent plants, breaking up the rock with a pick-axe to a fine rubble. This rubble then acts as a sponge, retaining moisture and giving a good hold to thirsty roots. Once plants get their roots down in this way they will grow strongly, often making exceptionally fine specimens.

Once the initial cultivation has been carried out it remains to choose only those plants which succeed on alkaline soils. Little lasting satisfaction comes from struggling to grow lime-hating plants on alkaline soils. It is far better to stick to known lime-lovers and enjoy the glorious healthy growth which will succeed your efforts. One or two misapprehensions exist, however, over which plants are in fact lime-haters. The rugosa roses, those strong-growing, free-flowering, shrubby roses from Japan, have sometimes been listed among those that dislike lime. This is very far from the truth. These lovely and useful roses will grow in alkaline clay, on shallow chalk or even in almost pure sand made chalky by the accumulated deposit of sea-shells. Such sites are often found in sandy patches near

the shore. As a general rule it is those plants with the strongest root systems that do best in chalk or lime soils. Hybrid tea roses of the 'Peace' family, strong-growing floribundas such as 'Queen Elizabeth', climbers such as the more vigorous H.T. sports: 'Climbing Shot Silk', 'Souvenir de Claudius Denoyal', and such strong grow-ing ramblers as 'Albertine', 'Emily Gray', 'Dorothy Perkins' and 'Débutante' are ideal.

Among perennials, too, it is the stronger growers that do best. The plume poppy, *Macleaya cordata,* paeonies of all kinds, asters, heleniums, pinks and carnations, *Stachys lanata,* the stately eremuri, the graceful feathery *Spiraea aruncus* will all succeed, provided the underlying hard pan has been broken up. Sun-lovers such as the artemisias with their decorative silvery leaves, cistus species, lavender, choisya,

rosemary and elaeagnus do well on shal-low, chalky soils; the sharp drainage making them hardier than they are else-where. Among shrubs and trees; lilacs, philadelphus, sorbus species, cotoneasters and chaenomeles are true chalk dwellers. On chalk and limestone they flower and fruit abundantly and their autumn colour

is often magnificent. Clematis, too, are natural lovers of alkaline places, but the large-flowered kinds need plenty of moist peat packed around their roots at planting time if they are to succeed. This technique gives wonderful results with dahlias, antirrhinums and petunias. Lupins and schizostylis are often said to be lime-haters but damp peat around their roots acts as a buffer as well as conserving the moisture they need and, given this treatment, they will do well.

Chalky soils are almost invariably alkaline and, in general, it is not possible to grow on them members of the heather family such as rhododendrons. Moreover, lime-induced chlorosis is common among many plants growing on chalky soil. Calcium has the effect of locking up certain minerals, particularly iron and manga-

nese, so causing the leaves to yellow (see Chlorosis). Heavy dressings of manure, compost and leafmould, all acid substances, are needed to counteract the soil alkalinity and to cure the chlorotic condition (see Chalky soils).

Most heaths, in common with rhododendrons and azaleas and other members of the family *Ericaceae,* sicken and die on

limy soils but the winter-blooming *Erica carnea* and its varieties as well as *E. mediterranea* and its hybrids will succeed, particularly if started in peat. Some magnolias, too, in particular *M. kobus, M.* × *loebneri, M. wilsonii* and *M.* × *highdownensis* will succeed and the rosy-purple *M.* × *lennei* does well in alkaline clay.

1 Candytuft, *Iberis amara,* **an annual of 9 to 12 inches**
2 *Sedum spectabile,* **a Chinese plant flowering in the autumn**
3 Hypericum or St John's Wort, an easy shrub to grow for its flowers and fruit
4 Verbascums flourish in chalky soils. They are apt to appear in unexpected places from self-sown seed
5 *Geranium renardii,* **a dwarf kind**

Plants for Chalky Soils

Herbaceous Perennials

Acanthus	Coreopsis	Helianthus	Papaver
Achillea	Dahlia	Helleborus	Primula
Anemone	(moist peat	Hesperis	(primrose and
(Japanese	round tubers)	Incarvillea	polyanthus)
anemones)	Dianthus	Inula	Pulmonaria
Anthemis	Doronicums	Iris (but not	Pulsatilla
Aster	Echinacea	I. kaempferi)	Rudbeckia
Aquilegia	Echinops	Kniphofia	Salvia
Aruncus	Eremurus	Limonium	Scabiosa
Bergenia	Eryngium	Linaria	Sedum
Campanula	Euphorbia	Lysimachia	Solidago
Centaurea	Galega	Macleaya	Stachys
Cephalaria	Geranium species	Nepeta	Thalictrum
Centranthus	Gypsophila	Oenothera	Verbascum
Chrysanthemum	Helenium	Paeonia	Veronica

Bulbs

Agapanthus	Crocus	Gladiolus	Narcissus
Allium	Eranthis	Iris	Nerine
Anemone	Fritillaria	Leucojum	Tulipa
(coronaria)	Galanthus	Lilium	Sternbergia
Colchicum	Galtonia	(some)	Zephyranthes

Shrubs and Trees

Acer	Corylus	Hebe	Pyracantha
(but not the	Cotoneaster	(Veronica)	Quercus
Japanese species)	Crataegus	Hibiscus	Rhus
Aesculus	Cryptomeria	Hippophae	Ribes
Amelanchier	Cupressus	Hypericum	Robinia
Aucuba	Cytisus	Ilex	Rosa species and
Berberis	(but not C.	Indigofera	strong growing
Betula	scoparius)	Jasminum	HTs and
Buddleia	Daphne mezereum	Juniperus	Floribundas
Buxus	Deutzia	Kerria	Rosmarinus
Caryopteris	Diervilla	Laburnum	Rubus
Ceanothus	Elaeagnus	Lavandula	Ruscus
Cedrus	Erica carnea vars.	Leycesteria	Sambucus
Ceratostigma	Erica darleyensis	Ligustrum	Senecio
Cercis	Erica mediterranea	Lonicera	Sorbus
Chamaecyparis	vars.	Malus	Spartium
(C. lawsoniana	Escallonia	Osmanthus	Syringa
and vars.)	Euonymus	Paeonia	Taxus
Chaenomeles	Fagus	(Tree paeonies)	Thuja
Chimonanthus	Forsythia	Philadelphus	Thujopsis
Choisya	Fraxinus	Phillyrea	Tilia
Cistus	Fuchsia	Pittosporum	Ulex

5

CHAPTER SEVEN
SHADE GARDENS

Shade plants

Garden shade can vary considerably in density and in its effect on the plants that are growing in it. It ranges from the really deep shade under large trees to the partial shade of a site that faces due east or west and get sunshine for at least half of the day.

The shade spread by a beech tree is very dense, but happily for us there is one group of enchanting plants which will tolerate this environment. These are the hardy cyclamen or sowbreads.

Cyclamen A valuable genus of dwarf tuberous plants, natives of the Mediterranean area, some flowering in autumn and early spring out of doors, others in the greenhouse or conservatory for winter decoration. Showy, neat and easy to cultivate, they belong to the same family as the primrose. Most species are on the borderline of hardiness in the British Isles, and whereas some flourish happily in sheltered gardens, the beauty of others may be best appreciated in an alpine house or cold greenhouse, or a sheltered sink garden or scree frame. In many species the flower stalk twists like a spring after the flowers have faded, to draw the seed capsules down to ground level.

C. neapolitanum (syn. *C. hederaefolium*), 4–6 inches, flowers range from pure white through pale pink to deep mauvish-pink, sometimes appearing as early as July, in warm damp weather, before the leaves; the flowering season proper is from September onward and the leaves are delightful and vary in shape and form, marbled with silver, splashed with pale cream or a lovely deep self green. They last throughout the winter forming good ground cover in extensive plantings. *C. orbiculatum* (syn. *C. atkinsii, C. coum, C. hiemale, C. vernum, C. ibericum*), 3–5 inches, rosy pink flowers starting in December and

going on until March, before the leaves appear (some authorities consider *C. coum*, 3 inches, with shorter flowering stems and magenta flowers early in the new year as a form). *C. repandum*, 4 inches, flowers scented, pink with darker mouth and carried well above the leaves, March to early May. Hardy in all districts.

Cultivation For the hardy species grown out of doors choose a loam rich in leaf-mould in partially shaded nooks of the

rock garden or turf bordering shrub borders or under trees, including conifers. Plant the tubers 1–2 inches deep and 4–5 inches apart in June or July, for the autumn-flowering kinds, and in September for the spring-flowering ones. *C. neapolitanum* needs to be planted a little deeper, say 3 inches. Protect with leaves or bracken in winter if necessary.

Among bulbs and perennials there are plenty of plants which like the shade that are well worth growing. Snowdrops, whether large or small, single or double, all appreciate some shade. So also does the snake's head fritillary, *Fritillaria meleagris,* and scillas of all kinds, together with the winter and summer snowflakes, *Leucojum vernum* and *L. aestivum.*

Wood anemones will make a delightful carpet under trees with their white and pale blue star-shaped flowers and *Cyclamen neapolitanum* and *C. repandum* are equally at home under trees or at the bottom of a shady hedge. Lilies-of-the-valley like woodland shade and act as excellent cover plants once naturalised.

Most lilies prefer a bed with shade around their roots and their heads in the sun. However, they do well in partial shade. In the herbaceous border, the shadier parts can be given up to the lovely species and varieties of hostas and helle-

If squirrels visit your garden protect the corms of cyclamen after planting. Spread wire netting over them just under the soil surface

There is a white form of Campanula latifolia which will show up well in shady conditions

bores. The former never display their magnificent foliage to such good effect when they are grown in full sunlight. The plants do well in bright sunshine but foliage is sacrificed to flower production.

Most modern strains of large-flowered polyanthus will adapt to full sunshine, but the flowers last a good deal longer and their colour fades less rapidly when the plants are grown in partial shade. Many annuals and biennials will flourish out of the sun, although the plants may be drawn up and the flowers washed out in colour. Some, however, do better in partial shade including mallows, foxgloves and honesty. Others, such as love-in-a-mist and nasturtiums, thrive equally well in sun or shade.

Where shady conditions are allied to a really damp soil, you can grow some strikingly exotic plants. Most ferns revel in moist shade and anyone able to meet their requirements should not fail to plant the stately royal fern, *Osmunda regalis,* which reaches a height of 6 feet or more when established. Other equally interesting plants in this respect are the lysichitums, with their enormous arum-like flowers and handsome paddle-shaped leaves, candelabra primulas such as *P. beesiana* and *P. pulverulenta,* the so-called giant rhubarb, *Gunnera manicata*, and most of the euphorbias.

Among the taller perennials with a preference for moist, shady spots are the goat's beard, *Aruncus sylvester,* with its feathery plumes of meadowsweet flowers, and *Artemisia lactiflora* with 5-foot spikes of creamy blossom which have a delicate vanilla-like fragrance.

Vinca major and *minor* also make good ground covers.

Cultivation The hardy periwinkles are useful trailing ground cover plants that flower best in the sun, but are quite happy in dry shade beneath a hedge or under

1 *Smilacina racemosa,* **the False Spikenard, has white flowers in May and red berries in autumn**
2 *Campanula latifolia* **prefers light shade**
3 *Fritillaria meleagris,* **Snake's Head**
4 *Cyclamen neapolitanum,* **a very hardy autumn flowering species from the Mediterranean area**
5 **Cyclamen are showy, neat and easy to cultivate. They belong to the same family as the primrose**
6 *Cyclamen coum* **flowers in late winter and early spring**
7 *Cyclamen coum* **is easily naturalised at the base of trees**
8 *Cyclamen repandum* **has scented flowers**

4

5

6

7

8

trees, in ordinary soil. Once planted leave them undisturbed and allow them to spread, cutting back when necessary in early spring. Propagation is by division or by digging up rooted layers in autumn or early spring. *V. rosea* may be grown in pots

of loam and peat; the tips of the shoots should be pinched out to encourage bushiness.

Violas do best in a moist, well-drained soil with light shade.

Large spreading trees such as oak or beech not only rob the soil at their feet of light, but also of both moisture and nourishment. In this kind of situation there are obviously few plants that will flourish successfully apart from certain shrubs such as the butcher's broom, *Ruscus aculeatus*. Its tiny spear-like, evergreen foliage (consisting not of leaves, but of cladodes, or flattened stems) makes a good show in the densest of shade. To enjoy the bright red berries of the butcher's broom, it will be necessary to plant both male and female forms.

An allied but lesser-known plant, *Danaë racemosa* (syn. *Ruscus racemosus*) the Alexandrian laurel, is equally tolerant of shade. Both of these shrubs are of modest dimensions. Neither will exceed much

more than 3 feet in height.

The common and Portuguese laurels will also grow well in dense, dry shade and make some of the finest shrubs for growing in the shadow of oak or beech. The Portuguese laurel, *Prunus lusitanica,* bears almond scented flower spikes and there are few finer evergreen shrubs for covert planting in dense woodland than the

1 *Viola gracilis*
2 Ferns of many kinds will naturalise, and meconopses flourish in shade
3 *Epimedium x warleyensis,* **a plant for shade, with coppery-red flowers**
4 *Magnolia liliflora nigra* **will grow satisfactorily in shade**
5 The white form of *Viola corruta,* **the Horned Violet, from the Pyrenees**
6 *Vinca major,* **the periwinkle, an evergreen plant useful for banks**

had a great vogue and plants were sold for £10 each. Now in certain coverts in southern England the plant has naturalised itself, easily ousting native woodland undershrubs.

Symphoricarpos (sim-for-i-carp-os) *S. albus* (syn. *S. racemosus*), snowberry, to 3 feet, although only introduced in 1817, now widely naturalised, spreading by means of runners and thriving in any situation; the large, white berries are conspicuous in autumn and winter; the best form is var. *laevigatus* which has also longer shoots, sometimes upwards of 6 feet.

Cultivation Few shrubs will thrive in such a variety of soils and situations, from full sun to deep shade. Plant from October to March in suitable weather. Prune in winter by cutting out the oldest wood and any dead wood. Propagation is

5

easily effected by division in winter or spring.

Symphoricarpos albus laevigatus, the snowberry, and many species and garden varieties of weigela also grow well in full shade. Other excellent shrubs include berberis, *Choisya ternata,* hypericums and *Olearia haastii.*

Given acid soil conditions *Rhododendron ponticum* will flourish in quite dense shade, although it will also need relatively moist soil. Most rhododendrons, however, thrive best in the light dappled shade at the fringes of woodland or that provided by the lacy foliage of silver birches, sorbus and similar trees. Camellias and magnolias also grow well in intermittent light and shade, which prevents petal scorch in hot, sunny weather and also protects buds and flowers from severe spring frosts.

common laurel, *Prunus laurocerasus,* with its handsome polished foliage and rapid rate of growth when established.

Another genus of berry-bearing evergreen shrubs, similar in appearance to those already mentioned are the aucubas. The most widely-grown species is the so-called Japanese laurel, *Aucuba japonica.* The variegated forms of this shrub were admired greatly in the last century and they make excellent shade plants. Like the laurels proper they are excellent as boundary hedges in shady conditions.

Their green and gold variegated leaves bring a feeling of sunshine to the darkest corners. As well as the type there are some splendid, named varieties, such as 'Goldenheart' in which the variegation is much more pronounced than in others. Both of these and the equally attractive green-leaved forms are dioecious (the flowers having one sex only), but they will bear berries freely if plants of both sexes are grown. Where moist humus is more plentiful the choice of suitable shrubs for dense shade becomes much wider. Evergreens such as buxus (box), skimmia, *Mahonia aquifolium* and *Viburnum tinus* (laurustinus) will all flourish. The partridge berries, *Gaultheria procumbens,* grow right to the foot of tree trunks, and species of sarcococca and the greater and lesser periwinkles, *Vinca major* and *V. minor,* also make good ground cover.

Mahonia (ma-ho-ne-a)

At one time the mahonias were included in the same genus *(Berberis)* as the barberries. The chief distinguishing character of these evergreen shrubs is the pinnate leaf (lacking in *Berberis*) and the fact that the leaves are spiny, while the branches lack spines. When *M. aquifolium* was first introduced from North America in 1823, it 6

Azaleas, both deciduous and evergreen species, also prefer dappled lighting to a position in full sun. Many shrubs that do well in sunny situation grow just as successfully in partial shade. Bamboos, the sweet pepper bush *Clethra alnifolia,* the red and yellow barked dogwoods (cornus), deutzia enkianthus, forsythias, potentillas, pyracanthas and yuccas are just a few of these.

Charming little plants for shade are **maianthemum.** A genus of two or three species only, related to *Smilacina.* They are hardy herbaceous perennials with creeping root-stocks, and racemes of small white flowers. The leaves are rather like those of the lily-of-the-valley *(Convallaria majalis)* and the flowers resemble those of the smilacinas. The maianthemums are useful colonisers of shady places, and once established will need little or no attention. *M. bifolium* is one of our rare native plants.

Cultivation No special care is needed, although shade from strong sun is desirable, and the plants thrive in thin woodland clearings. Detaching pieces of the creeping rhizomes provides a simple method of propagation (see also Smilacina).

Another pretty little thing is **smilacina.** With white flowers growing in a loose feathery spike atypical of the lily family, and with parallel-veined leaves.

Cultivation The soil should be a good loam, moist but not wet. Slightly shaded positions are preferred, in damp woodlands, on banks, in shrub borders or herbaceous borders. Planting is carried out in October or March. Propagation is by division of the roots in the same months as planting.

A plant which seeds itself freely in my garden is **tellima.** Said to be an anagram of *Mitella,* from which genus the genus was separated *(Saxifragaceae).* A genus of a single species, *T. grandiflora,* a hardy perennial woodland plant, resembling heuchera. It grows 1½–2 feet tall, and bears spikes of small, green, bell-shaped flowers, becoming reddish, in May and June. The leaves form a dome of heart-shaped, scalloped foliage, assuming bronze and ruddy tints in autumn. The plant comes from North America.

Cultivation Plant in autumn or early spring in ordinary garden soil in partial shade, or in a sunny position where the soil does not dry out. Propagation is by division in the spring, or by seed.

A plant I find useful in flower arrangements as well as a good ground carpeter is **lamium.** Dead nettle. Belonging to the dead nettle family, this herbaceous peren-

nial, from Europe and temperate Asia, is useful as ground cover where other plants, perhaps, would not grow.

Species cultivated *L. galeobdolon,* 1–1½ feet, yellow, June–July, a native plant; var. *variegatum,* white variegation on foliage L. maculatum, 8–12 inches, white central stripe on leaves, purple, pink or white flowers, summer, a native plant; var. *aureum,* golden leaves. *L. orvala,* 2 feet,

rosy-lilac, summer.

Cultivation Any garden soil will suit these plants, but *L. maculatum* does best in moist soils, lamiums can be planted in the autumn or spring and increased by division at any time of the year.

It's nice to have one plant which is so amenable and on which one can rely in a variety of circumstances.

Mahonia leaves dry well. Gather them as soon as they have turned colour

If you cut lamium for flower arrangements remove a little of the old stem with each piece. This takes water more easily

1 The white winter berries of *Symphoricarpos albus laevigatus*
2 The long racemes of sweetly scented flowers of *Mahonia japonica*
3 The leaves of *Mahonia bealii* colour well in autumn
4 The blue-black berries of *Mahonia aquifolium* are glaucous
5 Strawberry-like fruits of the dogwood *Cornus kousa* which enjoys light shade

CHAPTER EIGHT
SEASIDE GARDENING

Some of the prettiest gardens I know are at the seaside, but they could never have been made without forethought and sometimes even ingenuity.

There is a very wide range of plants for furnishing the sheltered seaside garden. Hybrid escallonias, cistus (in variety), hebes, tree lupins, *Spartium junceum, Lavatera olbia, Phlomis fruticosa,* hydrangeas, fuchsias, rosemaries and lavenders and all manner of grey-leaved shrubs which should include the cotton lavenders (santolinas), artemisias and helichrysums, all do well by the sea.

Perennial plants may include dianthus where there is lime, dimorphothecas, erigerons, geraniums (crane's-bills), echinops, eryngiums, kniphofias, limoniums (sea lavenders), armerias, sedums and mesembryanthemums.

Many shrubs and perennial plants, too tender for frosty inland districts, grow well by the sea when given protection from the worst sea-winds, though the range of plants for the colder maritime countries is necessarily more restricted. The almost constant enemies of seaside gardening are wind, salt and sand. Frost, however, is neither so prolonged nor so severe on the coast as it is inland, and seaside gardeners have been able to grow many frost-tender plants in the milder climate of their coastal gardens.

Salt can kill outright. Salt is carried in the spray and when this is caught up by the wind it is often deposited many hundreds of yards inland. Few plants are able to withstand the continual battering of sea-wind heavily charged with salt, which is heavily scorching to plants.

Sand-blast is often too lightly regarded by newcomers to the coast, though its effect can be quite as damaging as that of salt. Seashore gardens suffer badly from its searing effect when the wind picks up the sand from a nearby beach. Small seedlings are killed and adult foliage is

1 *Fatsia japonica,* an evergreen shrub
2 The 'mop head' hydrangeas do particularly well in exposed seaside localities
3 Lampranthus, members of the *mesembryanthemum* group, flourish by the sea on the far south-west
4 The frail-looking blooms of *Cistus purpureus*
5 One of the wall gardens at Rowallane, Northern Ireland, where many tender and interesting plants thrive
6 *Abelia grandiflora*
7 Gazanias make a good splash of colour during the summer months
8 Hebe 'Midsummer Beauty', a good shrub for seaside conditions

Coastal wind devastates plants. Only those with protection will escape stunting and deformity

Some of the best shelter trees, such as the maritime and Corsican pines, must be planted when only a foot high. They do not transplant well

bruised and blackened.

Many plants will grow only when given adequate shelter at the outset, and the planting of newly-made gardens exposed to the full ravages of gales off the sea is rarely successful without the aid of some artificial wind-screen.

Plantings of shelter belts of trees on a large scale benefit from an open fence of a two-bar wooden structure interwoven with foliage of gorse or spruce. For small gardens there is nothing better than a fence of wooden laths, one inch wide with spaces between of similar size, set vertically on a stout wooden framework and posts at either end for driving into the ground. Avoid a solid barricade such as a wall, which causes wind-turbulence on the lee side, since the aim is always to filter the

Plants which tolerate salt and wind are nowadays very largely selected from those grown in Australia and New Zealand. Shrubs that successfully resist salt-spray are planted facing the sea. These are often equipped with toughened leaves such as are found in the genus *Olearia*. *O. haastii* and *O. albida* stand any amount of salty wind. Others have shiny leaf surfaces.

Euonymus japonicus and *Griselinia littoralis* look bright and glossy within a few yards of the sea. Or the leaves of some may be coated with a gummy secretion as in *Escallonia macrantha*, enabling them to endure a coating of salt. Yet another form of protection is afforded by a multitude of tiny hairs which cover the leaf surfaces of grey-leaved and silver-leaved shrubs. It is a curious fact that most of these are well adapted to withstand the first brunt of a salty blast. Sea buckthorn, *Atriplex halimus*, *Senecio laxifolius* and *S. monroi* are among the best we have for prominent positions in exposed coastal districts. If sand-blast is a menace, tamarisk will grow with its roots in pure sand and is also useful for adding height to rough banks and walls.

Where there is room to plant, there is no lack of trees for providing shelter. Sycamore, willow and white poplar make use-

ful thickets close to the sea. This enables more worthwhile pines and cypresses to be grown, so that eventually there is a broad streamlined bank of vegetation sloping away from the sea, within the shelter of which many tender plants may thrive.

The best defence against wind is close planting and early thinning. In this way trees are protected when young by being planted close together. Small plants only should be used. These are less at the mercy of the wind and their roots suffer less.

The salt-laden gales which ravage coastal districts at intervals from October to mid-April are most harmful to plants. Therefore spring planting is advisable; this allows six months growing weather for plants to establish themselves.

1 *Convolvulus cneorum*
2 *Yucca gloriosa*
3 *Zantedeschia aethiopica* Crowborough a calla lily for shade
4 *Cytisus sessifolius,* a shrub for summer show in the seaside garden
5 *Ulex europaeus plenus*
6 *Agapanthus umbellatus*
7 The orange flowers of *Crocosmia x crocosmiiflora* make a useful display in the late summer and early autumn
8 *Garrya elliptica* has long silky green catkins during the winter months

7   8

Shrubs for colder maritime areas (cont.)

Berberis wilsonae
Buddleia davidii (in variety)
  B. globosa
Caragana arborescens
Caryopteris x clandonensis
Ceanothus x burkwoodii
  C. 'Cascade'
  C. 'Gloire de Versailles'
  C. 'Henri Defosse'
  C. 'Topaz'
  C. thyrsiflorus
Cistus corbariensis
  C. ladaniferus
  C. laurifolius
  C. populifolius
  C. 'Silver Pink'
Clematis flammula
Colutea arborescens
Coronilla glauca
  C. emerus
Cortaderia argentea
Cotoneasters (in variety)
Crataegus (in variety)
Cytisus battandieri
  C. scoparius hybrids
Elaeagnus ebbingei
  E. pungens aureo-variegata
Escallonia 'C. F. Ball'
  E. edinensis
  E. x langleyensis
  E. macrantha
Euonymus japonicus
Euphorbia veneta (E. wulfenii)
Garrya elliptica
Genista aethnensis
  G. lydia

G. hispanica
Griselinia littoralis
Hebe brachysiphon
  H. dieffenbachii
  H. 'Midsummer Beauty'
  H. salicifolia
Hibiscus in variety
Hippophaë rhamnoides
Hydrangeas (in variety)
Hypericum patulum 'Hidcote'
  H. androsaemum
Lavandulas (in variety)
Lavatera olbia rosea
Leycesteria formosa
Lonicera ledebourii
Lupinus arboreus
Lycium chinense
Medicago arborea
Olearia albida
  O. haastii
  O. macrodonta
Perovskia atriplicifolia
Phormium tenax
Pittosporum tenuifolium
Potentillas (in variety)
Prunus spinosa
Pyracanthas (in variety)
Ribes alpinum
  R. atrosanguineum
  Romneya x hybrida
Rosa rugosa (and its hybrids)
  R. spinosissima (and its hybrids)
Rosmarinus 'Miss Jessup's Upright'
  R. officinalis
Santolina chamaecyparissus
  S. incana

S. neapolitana
S. virens
Senecio laxifolius
  S. monroi
  Spartium junceum
Symphoricarpos orbiculata
  S. microphylla
Tamarix pentandra
Teucrium fruticans
Ulex europaeus plenus
Viburnum tinus
Yucca filamentosa

Some plants for seaside gardens (including tender kinds)

Agapanthus (species and hybrids)
Amaryllis belladonna
Aster pappei
Alstroemeria 'Ligtu Hybrids'
Convolvulus mauritanicus
Crambe cordifolia
Crinum (species and hybrids)
Crocosmia masonorum
Dimorphotheca barberiae compacta
  D. ecklonis
Gazanias
Kniphofias such as 'Maid of Orleans'
Mesembryanthemums
Montbretia (hybrids)
Myosotidium nobile
Odontospermum maritimum
Othonnopsis cheirifolia
x Venidio-arctotis
Zantesdeschia aethiopica

CHAPTER NINE
FLOWERS FOR FRAGRANCE

All women love scented flowers. My garden is full of fragrant plants, not all of them notable for their flowers alone, for some, such as myrtle, hyssop, rosemary, lavender and the many mints have scented foliage.

It is a perennial complaint of many gardeners that modern varieties of various plants, particularly roses, lack all or most of the fragrance of the older varieties. Some varieties are certainly much less fragrant than the 'old-fashioned' roses and a few seem to lack detectable fragrance, but, on the whole, a good modern variety will number fragrance among its qualities. Much depends, of course, upon the individual sense of smell, coupled with the 'scent memory' which all of us possess to some degree.

In general, it is true to say that, although the modern roses may be fragrant, the fragrance is lighter than that associated with the 'old-fashioned' varieties, which have returned to popularity in recent years, partly because of the rich, heavy fragrance of their blooms. Few gardens are too small to accommodate one or two of

1 On the Polesden Lacey estate, Surrey, famous for its trees, it is refreshing to find the cottage garden atmosphere among these roses
2 The flowers of this *Lilium auratum* hybrid are strongly scented
3 *Jasminum officinale* has heavily scented flowers in late summer
4 An attractive and highly fragrant combination of red roses and white regal lilies at Tintinhull House, Somerset
5 *Carpenteria californica,* a free-growing Californian shrub producing its large flowers in July. A sunny position is required. It was awarded the Royal Horticultural Society's First Class Certificate in 1888
6 A cottage garden in early summer when the fragrant rose 'Albertine' is at its best

Carpenteria deserves to be more widely grown, but it will not do well in urban areas. It resents atmospheric pollution

Lavender makes a good low-growing hedge

these; they may not have the perfectly-shaped blooms associated with the present-day hybrid tea varieties, but around mid-summer, and with some kinds, until late in the season, they will fill the garden with the true rose scent which, like all scents, is difficult to describe precisely, but is un-mistakable when it is found.

Just as distinctive is the true 'clove' fragrance of carnations. It is not, alas, found in every variety and sometimes those with the most shapely blooms lack fragrance entirely. Varieties as 'Dusky',

'Ice Queen' and 'Oakfield Clove' which possess it very strongly. It is also found in the 'Sweetness' hybrids, often treated as annuals, grown from seed sown in the spring, and producing single flowers in a good colour range.

It is usually possible to find a corner in which to plant a clump of lilies. But, again, it pays to be careful about the choice of species and varieties, for not all are fragrant, and some, such as the Turk's cap lily, *Lilium martagon*, have a decidedly unpleasant scent. Even among fragrant

5

6

1 *Choisya ternata* is one of the few Mexican shrubs that can be grown in the open in the south-east of Britain. It was introduced in 1825 and the fragrant flowers are plentifully produced in April and May. It is known as the Mexican orange blossom

2 *Chimonanthus praecox,* winter-sweet, a synonym of *C. fragrans,* best grown against a wall in full sun preferably near a path where the fragrance of the flowers can be savoured in later winter. The *grandiflorus* was given an Award of Merit in 1928

3 Nicotiana, the tobacco plant, is particularly fragrant at dusk

4 Corydalis lutea will readily naturalise in walls and flowers from April to October

5 The late Dutch honeysuckle is fragrant, particularly in the evening

6 *Philadelphus lemoinei* is one of the strongly fragrant mock oranges

types there is a great range of intensity of scent. Among those with the strongest and sweetest fragrance are the regal lily *(Lilium regale),* the Madonna lily *(Lilium candidum),* the golden-rayed lily of Japan *(Lilium auratum),* usually obtainable in its hardier form, *platyphyllum, L. henryi,* and 'Crow's Hybrids'.

Because they are more permanent than other plants, and need considerably less attention, flowering shrubs are becoming more and more popular. Where space is fairly limited it is worth while choosing some of those with fragrant flowers.

One of the prettiest little early flowering shrubs is corylopsis. Among those flowering in winter are such fine shrubs as *Hamamelis mollis,* the wych-hazel, with its yellow, cowslip-scented flowers, *Mahonia japonica,* its yellow flowers strongly fragrant, reminiscent of lily-of-the-valley, the sweetly fragrant white *Viburnum fragrans* and *V. tinus,* the old-fashioned but still excellent laurustinus. These are followed in spring by the native *Daphne mezereum,* the lilac-purple flowers of which are thickly clustered along the leafless twigs, the honey-scented, yellow azalea,

Rhododendron luteum, the double gorse, *Ulex europaeus plenus,* its golden flowers filling the air with the scent of vanilla, other viburnums including *V. × burkwoodii* and *V. carlesii* and the wisterias. Late spring brings the white flowers of *Choisya ternata,* the Mexican orange blossom and the lilacs with their refreshing, unmistakeable fragrance. These are soon followed by the mock oranges or philadelphus, their fresh, sweet scent of orange blossom. Among those with the strongest scent are the common *P. coronarius, P. delavayi,* the hybrid *P. × lemoinei* and the double-flowered 'Virginal'.

The sweet jessamine, *Jasminum officinale,* trained against a wall will bring its delicious fragrance through open windows, lavenders seem to give off their fragrance best on hot summer days, the spikes of buddleias attract the butterflies. The white or yellow flowers of the tree lupin, *Lupinus arboreus* are borne for most of the summer, as are the rich yellow peablooms of the Spanish broom, *Spartium junceum.*

The climbing honeysuckles come into flower in summer but carry the season on

1

2

The best time to plant chimonanthus is soon after it has flowered in February. Prune it at this time, cutting away most of the shoots that have flowered close to the base

Choisya will grow in any soil, including those containing chalk or lime. It prefers a sheltered position and will make a good and unusual hedge

well into the autumn. Again, not all are fragrant but those that are include the late Dutch honeysuckle, *Lonicera periclymenum serotina*, which is usually still producing its reddish-purple flowers in October.

Perennials which have flowers more or less fragrant include the sweet rocket, *Hesperis matronalis*, *Paeonia*, especially the old cottage garden *paeonias*, varieties of *P. officinalis*, border phloxes, *Astrantia*

carinthiaca fragrant, of all things, of marzipan, the perennial wallflower, *Cheiranthus* 'Harpur Crewe', the herbaceous clematis, *C. recta,* the border pinks and carnations, not all with the 'clove' scent described earlier, and, of course, many varieties of *Viola odorata,* the florist's violets, are exceptionally sweetly scented.

Of all the easily grown sweetly scented annuals surely the most popular are sweet peas. Modern varieties yield wonderful blooms for the minimum of trouble. Other familiar annuals are sweet alyssum, tobacco flower or nicotiana, night scented stock, mignonette, sweet sultan, pot marigold, snapdragon, marvel of Peru and cleome or spider flower.

Nothing scents the spring garden so well as the biennial wallflower, which mingles delightfully with the perfume of daffodils.

Taking them as a group, the bulbous plants include a good many fragrant plants, most of them fairly well known. The strong but pleasing fragrance of hyacinths is one of the qualities which make them so popular for early forcing in bowls; a few spikes in flower can fill the room.

There are also some fragrant greenhouse bulbs and it is certainly easier to appreciate their fragrance in such close confines than it is in the open air. Freesias, for instance, grown in pots, as they usually are, distil an indescribably sweet fragrance. Tuberoses *(Polianthes tuberosa)* are not grown as often as they were years ago, but the bulbs, or rather tubers, are obtainable from specialist suppliers and are well worth growing for the sake of the wonderful scent of the flowers in autumn and winter. Here, perhaps, is the place to bring in the lily-of-the-valley *(Convallaria majalis)* because it is so easily forced in boxes, or grown in pots, either for greenhouse use or for bringing into the living room when the plants are in flower. They can, of course, equally well be grown out of doors, particularly in a shady moist spot just as various other hardy fragrant plants such as Brompton stocks, lilacs, narcissus and lilies of various kinds, may either be grown outside or in pots in the greenhouse, usually flowering a little earlier, even when very little heat is available. Where more heat is available in winter it is possible to grow such fragrant flowers as stephanotis, acacias (usually mis-called mimosa), carnations, bouvardias, the little annual *Exacum affine,* gardenias, *Hoya carnosa, Jasminum polyanthum* and other tender jasmines, the jasmine-scented *Trachelospermum jasminioides,* the lily-scented *Datura arborea* as well as many others.

1 Sweet pea 'Bijou', a low-growing type which carries a good crop of flowers
2 'Hidcote', a deep, purple-blue form of *Lavandula spica,* useful for low-hedges

Although some seedsmen apply the term 'hardy annual' to many of the stocks, it is not advisable to give hardy annual treatment to any but the night flowering Matthiola bicornis

Rosa gallica is said to have been brought from Damascus by the Crusaders and hence known as the Red Damask

3 The deep pink flowers of *Rosa gallica* 'Surpass Tout' are fully double
4 *Rosa gallica* 'Cardinal Richelieu' has maroon flowers
5 The Tree lupin, a quick-growing shrubby plant, is delicately perfumed
6 The various types of stock have been derived from *Matthiola incana.* They can be obtained in various shades of pink and purple, and in white

CHAPTER TEN
PATIO PLANTS

Patio gardens

The patio, as a feature of our gardens, is a comparative newcomer to Britain although it has, for many years, been popular on the other side of the Atlantic. The word patio, in fact, is something of a misnomer; its original Spanish meaning referred to an *inner* court or enclosed space open to the sky, a feature commonly encountered in Spanish and South American houses.

Today, the description is applied to almost any kind of outdoor paved space adjacent to the house.

It can be a delightful feature allied to both house and garden and an ideal way both of displaying and caring for beautiful plants.

With many new houses, the patio becomes an integral part of the design, having been planned that way by the architect. This is a particularly satisfactory procedure, since it can be correctly sited to take full advantage of sun and shelter. At the planning stage, too, it is possible to arrange for an outdoor hearth with its flue connecting to those of the indoor fireplaces.

Plants on the patio should consist mainly of climbing and wall shrubs and any other plants suitable for growing in tubs, urns and other containers. Decorative tubs and jardinières are obtainable in terracotta and natural or artificial stone. Antique pots and figures are costly and increasingly hard to come by, but there are plenty of effective substitutes in artificial stone and other similar materials. Lead urns and cisterns, too, now sell for very high prices. It is possible, however, to obtain reproductions of old ones that are authentic in every detail, down to the grey-green patina that lead acquires with age and exposure to weather. Even these are not exactly cheap, but their cost is only a fraction of that of the genuine article.

Several shapes and sizes are available from terrace type pots which are large enough to hold small shrubs or a mass of bedding plants to bulb bowls and troughs. They are ideal containers for the woman gardener as they are light and pleasant to handle. They must be used with care, however, as they are fairly fragile when filled. For example, it is not wise to pull a large trough, when filled, by its rim, as this can break off easily. A long trough must be supported underneath with a piece of timber if it has to be moved when filled. Usually, however, containers should be placed in their correct positions first and then filled and planted.

Some window-box or plant trough designs are manufactured from strong plastic

materials which result in lightweight, rot-proof articles. They also have particular appeal to the woman gardener as they are attractively decorated by relief designs. Suitable plastic and fibreglass shallow plant troughs can be obtained for indoor use. These are ideal for placing pot plants in, especially on the window ledge. A few small pebbles in the bottom plus a regular supply of small amounts of water will provide the ideal moist atmosphere for growing many plants. There are several fibreglass plant tubs on the market. These are made from special high-quality fibreglass in various colours, such as red, yellow and green. The material used in their construction is light, so the containers are easy to handle. As their colouring is permanent, there is no need to paint them and they will not rot or warp.

Fibreglass is also used for troughs, window-boxes, urns and other types of plant container.

Plants grown on the walls adjacent to the patio are best grown in beds. This, however, may not always be practicable because of damp courses, drains or other constructional hazards. But many climbers will do quite well in tubs or boxes. Although their rate of growth may be slowed down considerably, this is not necessarily a disadvantage, as it enables a greater variety of plant to be grown.

1 Flowering and foliage plants grown in urns, ornamental vases, plant boxes of many kinds, tubs and large pots, will all help to furnish the balcony garden

2 Rectangular tiles make a clean path to the house

3 *Fuchsia fulgens,* a greenhouse species, has long, coral-scarlet flowers

4 Fuchsia 'Burning Bush' looks effective when planted in a large container. The pale yellow-green foliage, with red veins and stems, is a good foil for the coral-magenta flowers

5 Round units are used to pave this patio. Plants in pots and in beds surrounded by a low wall provide colour

6 Fuchsia, 'Beauty of Bath', a free-flowering hardy cultivar.

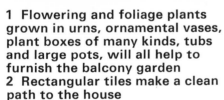

Actual plants used will depend largely on the tastes of the gardener. The following suggestions are based on experience of what will grow well and happily on a patio and give the pleasure of long-lasting colour. Marigolds (calendulas and tagetes), Virginian stocks *(Malcolmia maritima)*, campanulas, nasturtiums *(Tropaeolum majus)*, annual or China asters (callistephus), lobelias, nemesia, Busy Lizzie (impatiens), wallflowers (cheiranthus), petunias, forget-me-nots (myosotis), pansies, arabis, periwinkle, (vinca), pelargoniums, London Pride *(Saxifraga umbrosa)*, stonecrops (sedums) and houseleeks (sempervivums), crocuses, dwarf tulips, daffodils and hyacinths, antennaria, zinnias, mesembryanthemums, dwarf antirrhinums and many more. All are comparatively low growing and all are easy.

In winter, patio gardens just cannot be a blaze of colour, but the troughs and pots need not be empty. Winter-flowering heathers (*Erica carnea* and others), variegated ivies (hederas), aucuba, dwarf conifers, skimmia, some of the hypericums, *Osmanthus delavayi, Mahonia aquifolium, Senecio laxifolius,* some of the pernettyas and a small camellia or two are all worth growing where there is space.

There are certain top favourites as one would expect and fuchsias are one of these Window boxes look decorative when filled with such varieties as 'Benitchea', 'Evening Sky', 'Santa Lucia', 'Sicna Blue', 'Tinker Bell', because they cascade slightly over the sides of the box.

Because I love scented plants I grow

1 Round slabs, used in conjunction with infilling pieces, are used to pave this patio garden
2 A formal patio where a dripping fountain provides a sense of coolness
3 Well-stocked plant tubs on a brick-paved terrace
4 Heliotrope, 'Cherry Pie', a summer flowering plant grown for its perfume
5 A 'Chilstone' reproduction of a Regency basket plant container
6 Concrete slabs are used in contrasting colours to provide a formal pattern for this patio

Plant containers made from polystyrene rapidly assimilate warmth. This keeps the compost in them much warmer than in clay or stone pots

Old wine barrels sawn in half make excellent tubs. To make drainage holes in the base use a red hot poker

heliotrope, which is easily raised from seed. By taking cuttings in autumn or spring a supply of small plants for pot work or for bedding out of doors can be maintained, autumn rooted cuttings usually making the better plants. Pinch out the tops when about 5 inches of growth has been made to produce bushy plants. Water frequently and feed before flowering. Standard heliotropes are obtained by stopping at the desired height and side shoots stopped subsequently to form a head.

So, for complete success you need the right plants and the right soil. More about both these subjects in the next section.

WINDOW BOXES

1

2

3

Fixing A window-box on a high sill that is not securely fixed can be dangerous, so use long hasps and staple fittings to secure the box to the window frame. It is better to prepare the box actually sited on the window ledge, as this saves carrying a box full of soil to the ledge and siting it in what is often an awkward position. Lay broken crocks on the bottom of the box at about $\frac{1}{2}$ inch deep to prevent soil being washed out of the drainage holes and at the same time give adequate drainage. On top of this a fibrous material such as peat should be laid at a depth of 2 inches. To within a $\frac{1}{2}$ inch of the rim the soil proper should be John Innes No 2, or you can mix up 3 parts loam (or good garden soil), 1 part of peat or leafmould and 1 part of sharp sand. To each bushel add two or three handfuls of bonemeal. The soil should be changed every two or three years, or the top two or three inches should be replaced with fresh soil or compost.

Planting Pelargoniums or fuchsias, in association with alyssum or lobelia, together with foliage plants, such as coleus, or the grey-leaved *Senecio cineraria,* will provide a summer display requiring little maintenance. Hardy and half-hardy plants, including stocks, zinnias and verbenas, all give a long-lasting display if the dead flowers are picked off regularly. Tobacco plants, French and African marigolds also make a good effect.

Begonias (both tuberous and fibrous-rooted species), ferns, fuchsias, creeping Jenny *(Lysimachia nummularia)* with periwinkles, *Tradescantia fluminensis,* and the smaller ornamental ivies, are suitable for a north-facing aspect. Where there is partial shade only (north-east and north-west aspects) begonias, pelargoniums, lobelia, alyssum and phacelias all do well. Climbing plants should be planted at the ends of the box and allowed to climb up the walls on either side of the window with suitable supports.

Climbing nasturtiums will cling to strings or wires, *Ipomoea rubrocaerulea* 'Heavenly Blue' (morning glory) likes a sheltered, sunny position.

More permanent climbers are the compact ivies, such as *Hedera helix aureo-variegata* or the smaller-leaved 'Buttercup'. Vines, also the Virginian creeper, *Parthenocissus quinquefolia,* or the smaller-leaved, more compact *P. henryana,* *Vitis vinifera purpurea* and *V. coignetiae* are all suitable.

Bulbs One of the best times of year for a window-box is early in the year when daffodils, tulips, hyacinths, scillas, chionodoxas and other bulbs are flowering.

Hardwood window boxes can be oiled or varnished. Softwoods should be treated with preservatives (never creosote) or can be painted

Timber for window boxes should be at least $\frac{1}{2}$ inch thick and the inside depth should be from 7 to 10 inches

4

1 A well planted window-box
2 Pelargoniums make fine window-box decoration
3 A window-box planted for summer effect with coloured foliage plants requires a minimum of attention
4 Because of their exposed situations some balconies will need protection from wind. It is often possible to glass in one end of the balcony to provide shelter
5 Balcony gardens can be made colourful in summer by using annual plants

5

CHAPTER TWELVE
HANGING BASKETS

Hanging baskets

I wonder who first thought of making a hanging basket? What decorative little gardens these are, and yet we often see those that havn't quite come off. I have studied them for some years and it is apparent that many people do not realise that a beautiful hanging basket does not just happen. Like the other types of gardens already discussed (window boxes and patio containers) none must be neglected. It is essential to use good soil of a proper texture and rich in humus and nutrients. I have also noticed that the loveliest hanging baskets are always those which are in shade during some part of the day, the best being those shaded from the mid-day sun.

The use of hanging baskets is a simple but very attractive way of decorating a porch 'or terrace during the summer. Baskets may also be hung from the rafters of a greenhouse, for decoration during most of the year. They can be bought in varying sizes, from 10–18 inches in diameter and 6–9 inches deep.

Baskets are made of stout galvanised wire in an open mesh or a wave design or of green, plastic-coated, rustproof wire, in the same patterns. Polythene Baskets are also available in green, red, white, yellow and blue and baskets made entirely of alkathene can be purchased with a special drainage device. In greenhouses, square wooden containers made of slats are often used, particularly for orchids of trailing habit, such as *Stanhopea*.

For safety's sake baskets should be hung from strong hooks, well above eye level where they cannot obscure the light or a view or be knocked about as people pass under them.

Planting up the basket For outdoor use plant up during the latter half of May or very early June, wedging the basket in the top of a large bucket, bowl or box to hold it firm while the planting is, done. Line it with damp sphagnum moss; about half a gallon of this will be required to make a good lining. Alternatively thickish polythene can be used to line the basket, when holes will need to be punched in the base for drainage although it is possible to purchase perforated polythene which is quite suitable. Polythene does not look as decorative as sphagnum moss but holds the moisture better and if the basket cannot be given daily attention it is probably better to use this material, although a thin layer of peat packed within the sphagnum moss lining will help considerably with water retention.

If sphagnum moss is not available, hay packed tightly round the interior of the

basket, is an adequate substitute.

Some gardeners like to put a small plastic saucer in the base to catch and retain some of the water, and to reduce drip to some extent.

A reasonably rich compost is best because the small amount that can be accommodated has to provide sustenance for a fairly extensive root system. John Innes potting compost No. 2 is suitable, especially if a little leafmould is incorporated. Do not attempt to get too many plants into one basket. A 12 inch diameter basket will hold three plants from 5 inch pots, plus several smaller or trailing plants between them and around the edge.

Choose plants that are just coming into flower, turn them out of their pots and fill the well of the basket with compost, firming it with the fingers. Place the larger plants in position, angling them slightly towards the edge. At this stage small plants such as lobelia and alyssum can be tucked between the mesh of the basket so that eventually the flowers will clothe the sides. Continue to pack in the soil round the root balls and make it firm, leaving a slight depression or well on the

surface of the soil, another trick to conserve moisture and to prevent water from overflowing when the basket is watered. The surface should be about 2 inches below the rim of the basket. Seeds of nasturtiums can be pushed into strategic positions at this stage. Immerse the basket in water, then allow it to drain before hanging it up.

In an unheated greenhouse far more

elaborate baskets can be planted up during early May. The baskets are lined and filled with compost and carefully inverted on the staging, when young plants of coleus, chlorophytum or tolmiea can be pushed through the structure of the basket and firmed with a dibber. Leave the basket in this position for two or three weeks before turning it right way up and planting up the rest of it in the usual way. The ideal way of holding a basket partially prepared in this way while the remaining planting is done is to construct a triangle of laths which can be laid over a bin to wedge the basket without damaging the plants already there. It will be necessary to scoop out some of the compost before planting up the top. Water very thoroughly, while the basket is still in the planting position.

Maintenance Avoid position in full sun or deep shade; the former dries out the arrangement too quickly and the latter discourages showy flowering, although such positions are suitable for baskets planted up with ferns for foliage effect. Water three or four times a week, daily or even twice daily during very hot weather, adding a flower fertiliser to the water at the recommended rate once a week, after flowering has started. Water from above, allowing the basket to drain if possible to

To reach a hanging basket with a hose tie it to a cane

Plastic hanging baskets with a built-in drip tray are now available. These simplify watering and feeding

avoid leaching out the plant food; otherwise immerse it for a few minutes in a tub of water and allow surplus to drain away before hanging it up again.

Watering a hanging basket from above can be difficult unless one stands on steps. It can, of course, be lifted off its hook but a large basket full of earth and plants can be quite heavy and awkward. Two methods of dealing with this problem are worth mentioning One is to fix a small pulley in place of the hook. Strong cord, or preferably strong pliable wire or chain, is fixed to the suspension ring of the basket and passed over the pulley. The other end is attached to a roller blind hook fixed on the nearest wall. The basket may then be lowered for watering and easily raised again. The other method is to use a device, obtainable commercially, known as a 'Tommy Longarm'. Basically this is a small watering can mounted on a swivel on the end of a long pole. A length of string fixed to the can runs through a hook and

down the pole. Pulling on the string tips the can thus enabling the basket to be watered easily from below. Wash the leaves occasionally and snip off dead flower heads to keep a well-groomed appearance.

Suggested plants The following is a list of plants suitable for basket cultivation. Those marked (G) are more suitable for *Flowering plants for summer display:* Achimenes; Ageratum; Begonia 'Gloire de Lorraine' and pendulous kinds such as 'Mrs Bilkey', 'Fleur de Chrysantheme', 'Golden Shower', 'Lena', 'Meteor'; *Begonia semperflorens* for mild localities; Calceolaria; *Campanula isophylla* and *C. isophylla alba*; *Chrysanthemum frutescens* (marguerite); *Columnea banksii* (G); Fuchsia, drooping varieties such as 'Cascade', 'Golden Marinka', 'La Bianco', 'Marinka', 'Thunderbird'; Heliotrope; *Hoya bella* (G); *Lantana camara* for mild localities; *Lebelia pendula* and *L. tenuior*; *Lobularia maritima* (sweet Alison); Pelar-

gonium, upright zonal kinds for top of basket, ivy-leaved varieties for draping the sides, such as 'Abel Carriere', 'Edward VII', 'Galilee', 'L'Elegance', 'Madame Crousse', 'Madame Morrier'; Petunia especially 'Balcony Blended' strain; Tropaeolum (nasturtiums), especially climbers or trailers; Verbena, dwarf and trailing. *Perennials:* Aubrieta; *Campanula portenschlagiana; Cerastium tomentosum; Cymbalaria muralis; Glechoma hederaefolia; Lysimachia nummularia; Vinca minor. Foliage plants: Adiantum cuneatum* (G); *Adiantum gracillimum* (G); *Asparagus sprengeri* (G); Chlorophytum (G); Coleus (G); *Davallia canariensis* (G); Hedera (ivy) in variety; *Nephrolepis exalta* (G), *Nephroelpis fosteri* (G), *Saxifraga stolonifera* (syn. *S. sarmentosa*); Smilax (G); *Tolmiea menzisii* (G); *Tradescantia fluminensis* (G); Zebrina in variety (G). *Bulbs:* (for late winter and spring display) Crocus, *Narcissus* (daffodil), *Galanthus* (snowdrop), Tulip (double).

1 A small hanging basket, planted with fuchsias and pelargoniums
2 Ivy-leaved pelargoniums are ideal for providing a showy basket
3 A floriferous begonia in a basket
4 Browallia, a greenhouse flowering annual, makes a decorative trailing plant for a hanging basket

3

4

CHAPTER THIRTEEN
MINIATURE GARDENS

Miniature gardens

The prettiest gardens are not always the biggest neither are the keenest gardeners found only in large gardens.

Where space is really limited, there is only one answer. Design and planting must be scaled down to fit the area available. But gardening on this reduced scale can be just as rewarding. In these pygmy plots, the opportunity for healthy exercise may be lacking, but to many gardeners, especially the elderly and those who prefer to 'potter', this may not necessarily be a great disadvantage.

Miniature gardens can take a number of forms. In the very small plot, you can share the pleasures of those who work on a broader canvas by restricting your planting, not only to single specimens of your favourite plants, but also by growing those that are compact in habit with a slow rate of increase.

The miniature garden proper, however, will not be able to rely on such measures. For its impact, it will have to depend mainly on dwarf plants, some of which may be miniature replicas of their taller counterparts while others will display their own individual characteristics.

Fortunately there are many small forms of familiar and lovely flowering plants. They include shrubs of many kinds including lavender, azaleas, rhododendrons and ericas and little violas, anchusa, hardy geraniums, irises and many bulbs.

Miniature rose gardens Miniature roses have become generally popular in recent years. One of their main attractions lies in the opportunity that they afford of enjoying the beauty of roses where space would not permit the planting of a rose garden of the orthodox kind.

Sometimes known as fairy roses, many of these delightful dwarfs bear a strong resemblance to popular hybrid tea roses and floribundas. Others have equally delightful individual characteristics.

Little interest was shown by gardeners in these pygmy roses until after World War II, when scarcity of garden help and a swing from houses to flats and maisonettes brought their many useful qualities into prominence. These, apart from their compact habit, include permanence and a very long flowering season.

Many of the miniature roses stem from the dainty *Rosa rouletti,* a tiny rose that was discovered in a Swiss cottage garden by a Dr. Roulet and named in his honour. From this charming miniature have evolved, directly or indirectly, many of the loveliest miniatures available today, including 'Tom Thumb', 'Pixies' and 'Midget'.

Miniature roses are extremely hardy. They come into flower early—often by the middle of May—and continue to produce their flowers throughout the summer and autumn. They are best planted from pots as they do not like root disturbance. This makes it possible to plant them at almost any time of year although March and April are the best months for this operation. Those planted in summer should be given plenty of water during dry spells in their first season.

The many named forms now available can be used to create a complete rose garden in miniature or can be incorporated as a separate feature of a larger garden. They are also useful for permanent dwarf bedding schemes.

All the features of a full-sized rose garden can be incorporated, scaled down, of course, to suitable dimensions. Pygmy pergolas, trellises and small rustic screens can be used to support climbing varieties, while miniature standards will emphasise focal points and act as central features of miniature bedding schemes.

Raised beds in a tiny garden bring plants nearer eye level

Many alpine or rock garden plants are ideal for little gardens. Many grow flat on the ground and do not need rocks

Among those most widely grown are 'Baby Gold Star' (golden yellow), 'Bit O' Sunshine' (gold), 'Humoreske' (deep pink), 'Little Buckaroo' (scarlet with white centre), 'Sparkle' (single scarlet) and the midget rose that started it all, *Rosa rouletti*.

'Baby Masquerade', a newer introduction, is a perfect replica, in miniature, of the favourite floribunda of the same name, with clusters of flowers that produce the typical kaleidoscope of colour of the latter.

This rose, together with 'Cinderella' (pale pink edged white), 'Coralin (coral-pink) and 'Maid Marion' is obtainable in standard form. There are climbing forms of the bright pink 'Perla Rosa', the yellow and orange 'Little Showoff', which is practically perpetual-flowering and 'Baby Crimson', which is also known as 'Perla d'Alcanada'. 'Pink Cameo', too, makes an attractive climber. None of these climbing miniatures exceeds 4–5 feet in height.

A good way of getting horticultural quarts into pint pots is to garden in sinks and troughs. Several of these plant containers, each with its separate planting scheme, can be accommodated in a minimum of space. Many a town forecourt, backyard or balcony could benefit from the inclusion of a feature of this kind.

Unfortunately, genuine stone troughs

Miniature roses need only a minimum of attention where pruning is concerned. This operation is best carried out with a sharp pair of nail scissors. It consists mainly of removing weak growths and cutting back dead or diseased shoots to healthy wood. It is carried out in spring.

These small roses thrive best in similar types of soil to those in which the hybrid tea roses and floribundas do well. They like a fairly heavy, slightly acid loam, rich in humus. Lack of humus can be remedied by forking in well-rotted animal manure or garden compost, a few weeks before planting. If neither of these is available, peat or leafmould, laced with bonemeal, make satisfactory substitutes.

These dwarf roses will also flourish and look well in the old stone troughs already mentioned; the sinks are too shallow and there would be a danger of the roots drying out. They can be used, as well, for another kind of miniature garden, the window box, provided that the latter is at least 9 inches deep.

1 Miniature gardens made up of saxifrages, sedums, campanulas, arenarias, lewisias and miniature conifers
2 Androsaces, houseleeks, lewisias, dwarf conifers and other alpine plants make an interesting small garden
3 A permanent rock garden in a miniature can be established in stone trough or sink
4 Although bonsai trees such as this have the appearance of great age, it is possible, by careful training, to produce specimens in a few years. Many trees may be trained in this way, both deciduous and evergreen

and sinks are fast becoming collectors' items and, in consequence, increasingly difficult and expensive to come by. The stone sinks of Victorian kitchens and sculleries have long ago been replaced by vitreous enamel and stainless steel, while the larger troughs, formerly used for watering cattle and horses, have given place to galvanised iron tanks.

The occasional specimen still turns up at country sales and in junk yards, but dealers are aware of their value and prices have risen astronomically. As an alternative, concrete or old glazed sinks can be adapted for the purpose. But neither of these will have the charm of the genuine article which, if it has been out-of-doors for any length of time, will be weathered and decorated with mosses and lichens.

Particular attention must be paid to drainage before planting up any of these containers. A piece of perforated zinc should cover the existing drainage hole and the base of the trough or sink should be covered with broken crocks or stone chippings to a depth of 2–3 inches. On top of this goes a layer of peat moss or chopped turves, the latter grass side down.

The planting mixture should consist of 2 parts of loam to 1 part of peat and 1 of sharp sand, with a dusting of lime or the addition of mortar rubble. The lime content must be omitted where ericaceous plants, dwarf rhododendrons, or other lime-haters are to be planted.

Among the many plants that can be grown successfully in a sink or trough garden are the hardier small saxifrages, sempervivums (houseleeks), thrift and other alpine plants of tough constitution. In a shady situation, mossy saxifrages, hardy cyclamen and miniature ferns will flourish.

For more permanent effects, use can be made of some of the dwarf shrubs and conifers mentioned below.

One way of entering a new world of gardening, is to train the eye to new visions and the fingers to new skills by cultivating bonsai.

Bonsai

The Japanese word *bonsai* literally means 'planted in a shallow vessel', but it is now usually restricted to trees or shrubs artificially dwarfed.

The Japanese have a great number of 'styles' for bonsai, including some which combine several specimens, and books or the subject will also illustrate some ingenious 'short cuts' such as laying a sapling down horizontally to make it produce vertical shoots which are then dwarfed.

Remember that a bonsai specimen is not just a stunted tree: it is a work of art only achieved after years of almost daily attention.

1

The ideal bonsai tree is one which has been naturally dwarfed in the wild state, perhaps growing in a rock cranny or in a very exposed position. The Japanese prize such trees very highly, all the more as infinite care and patience is needed to extract them, which might be done over several months. The Japanese also air-layer rugged or unusually shaped portions of tree branches.

The normal method of producing a bonsai tree, however, is to start with seed, seedlings or rooted cuttings. Seedling trees can be found in the countryside, and those

1 Deficits of rainfall can be made up by watering, and 'artificial rain' provides a gentle supply of water over a long period.
2 Dwarf conifers of many kinds are ideal for miniature gardens
3 At the RHS Garden, Wisley, there is a splendid collection of trough gardens, each one planted up in an individual way with succulents and miniature conifers
4 One of the troughs, which contains a selection of houseleeks

2

Watering bonsai is vital. In hot, dry weather plunge the tree and its container under water until bubbles cease to rise from the soil surface. This will ensure that the soil is evenly moist

A fine spray of clean water over the foliage will do much to refresh the tiny trees on a summer day

which are naturally stunted or unusually shaped form good starting points. Almost any kind of tree or shrub can be used, though conifers are probably the easiest to train. (Naturally dwarf forms of conifers are not suitable for bonsai as they seldom respond to training.)

The points to aim at in a bonsai tree are that it should be aesthetically pleasing and well proportioned—mere distortion is not the aim. It should have a stout trunk, and the root growth and top growth must be in balance.

Growing from seed allows complete control over the whole process. Seed should be fresh and is sown in shallow pans or boxes of sandy loam, placed in a cold frame or in a cool place outside shaded from sun. Germination sometimes takes a long time, but once the seedlings appear and are an inch or two high they should be transferred to individual small containers. Small flowerpots or waxed paper containers (e.g. ice-cream tubs punctured with drainage holes) can be used, and a popular method is to plant in a dried half-orange or grapefruit skin. It is important to prevent the containers from drying out.

During the first year root pruning will be needed once, or possibly twice. If the plant is in an orange skin or a carton the roots will grow through and should be cut off as they appear. Plants in pots must be taken out and any long thick roots cut right out, the fibrous roots being trimmed lightly. The purpose of root pruning at any stage is not to weaken the plant but to encourage the formation of a mass of active roots in a small space.

Any vigorous-growing shoots that appear should be pinched out with finger and thumb, though too many leaves must not be removed at once.

In the second season the young tree grows rapidly and needs constant attention: this season really determines the success of the final product. The roots need cutting back in spring and in midsummer, preceding this by the picking away of some of the soil with a pointed stick. After root trimming repot very firmly in the same container, adding fresh compost.

In the third year the tree can be placed in its permanent container, which should be glazed and relatively shallow. From this time on a spring root trim is sufficient, but unwanted shoots must be continually pinched out as they appear. Keep the ultimate desired shape of the bonsai firmly in mind, achieving this not only by pinching but if necessary by wiring the branches with very soft wire spiralled around them, or by weighting or tying down the branches. Crowded or crossing branches should be avoided.

The annual trim and repotting is an opportunity to lift the tree out of the soil a little each time, exposing the base of the trunk and the upper roots. Shade from direct sun is desirable, but the trees need plenty of light and air and of course adequate water. A little weak liquid fertiliser may be given every two or three weeks in the growing period, especially in the early years.

Suitable soil mixtures are as follows: Deciduous trees: 6 parts of loam, 2 parts of old rotted leafmould, or peat, 1 part of course sand. Conifers: 6 parts of loam, 1 part of leafmould or peat, 3 parts of coarse sand. John Innes potting compost can be used if necessary, adding more sand for conifers.

3

4

CHAPTER FOURTEEN
WINDOW SILL PLANTS (INDOORS)

To me there is a great difference between house and windowsill plants. In the first group there are those which will grow in many places in the home. The others need a high light intensity, though not necessarily strong and direct sunlight. They are in fact those plants which are usually grown or raised in a greenhouse but which will tolerate the dryer conditions of a living room.

Cyclamen

Many people begin this kind of gardening by being given a plant, a cyclamen for instance. Water moderately and feed weekly with a liquid feed throughout the flowering period which, with a selection of plants, can be from November to March. Remove old blossoms and leaves by tugging them out from the base of the stem. After flowering, gradually dry off, resting the tubers out of doors in a dry frame or plunge bed during the summer months.

In August soak the pot and tuber that have previously been dried off all summer and once the tiny leaves begin to sprout, repot in a fresh compost of 2 parts of loam to 1 part of leafmould and sand. The tuber should be potted so that the level of the soil surrounds its circumference, no deeper. Keep close for a few days until growth starts again. Syringe daily, keep the plants shaded and maintain a moist atmosphere and temperature of 55–60°F (13–16°C).

Propagation is from seed sown in very fine compost between mid-August and mid-November in a temperature of 50–60°F (10–16°C). Prick off the seedlings and then pot them into thumb pots. Subsequently pot them on, with the necks of the tubers well above soil level.

Coleus Every year I raise some coleus from seed in pans on a warm windowsill. I love the gorgeous colours of the plants.
Cultivation Use John Innes potting compost in 5–6 inch pots. Keep adequately warm and moist. Summer temperatures, 60–65°F (16–18°C), winter, 55°F (13°C), minimum, 45°F (7°C). Water well during the warm season, less so during the cooler months. Weak liquid feeding is beneficial throughout summer. Propagation is by seed sown in February, March and April,

1 Modern strains of cyclamen produce large elegant blooms on strong stems
2 This group shows the sturdy growth and the wide variety in colour of cyclamens
3 There are many forms of *Coleus blumei,* all grown for their brilliantly coloured leaves
4 The double-flowered begonias 4 and 5 are examples of the large-flowered hybrids. 'Flamingo' 6 is one of a number of *Begonia semperflorens* types often used for summer bedding. The Rex Begonias 7 are grown for their colourful leaves

Tuberous begonias must be gradually dried out after they have flowered. Leave them in their pots, store in a frost-proof shed or knock them out and store in clean, dry sand

Coleus shoots will root in water. They can then be potted to make new plants

barely covered in a temperature of 70°F (21°C), or by cuttings of young shoots taken at almost any time. Stop young plants by pinching out the growing point to induce bushiness.

Begonia These are deservedly popular plants, whether the foliage or the flowering kinds.

The genus begonia is usually divided into two groups; those species with fibrous roots and those with tubers. Other classifications give special treatment to the winter-flowering forms, and to those grown exclusively for the interest of their leaves. A notable feature of begonias is their oblique, lop-sided or uneven sided leaves.

Cultivation The fibrous-rooted begonias are usually obtained from seed, which should be sown in January in a temperature of 60°F (16°C). It is also possible to root growths from the base of the plant. The sub-shrubby perennial forms will come easily from normal cuttings, or all begonias may be raised by leaf cuttings.

Most begonias need a winter temperature of about 60°F (16°C). The ornamental Rex type must not be exposed to full sun-

6

4

5

7

1

2

3

4

light, and many of the other classes will be happy with much less light than suits other greenhouse plants.

The tuberous begonias are usually started into growth by placing them in shallow boxes of peat or leafmould in February or March, hollow side uppermost, in a temperature of 60–70°F (16–21°C). After roots have formed the tubers are potted up in small pots and later moved into larger ones.

Do not start to feed these tuberous plants till they have formed roots, or they will decay, but after they are rooted a bi-weekly dose of liquid manure is helpful. The tuberous begonias may also be raised from seed, and if this is sown in February plants may flower from July to October.

Epiphyllums I get tremendous delight from my few epiphyllums or leaf-flowering cacti. They give wonderful flowers without much trouble.

Cultivation These plants are easily grown and will thrive in almost any type of compost. Encourage new growth each year as this will flower more freely. Repot plants when they become potbound, water them freely from April to September. Keep them in the greenhouse in winter and spring, but place them out of doors for summer. Plants do not like too strong sunshine.

Until recently only a comparatively limited range of colours was available, but these plants have responded to plant breeding in a most exciting way. Other colours from the species are now available from specialist growers. Our pictures tell their story.

These plants grow quite large, but there are smaller species, rhipsalis and the popular zygocactus or Christmas cactus.

By crossing epiphyllum 1 'London Magic' with 3 'London Glory' the unpredictabliity of seedlings from hybrid parents is demonstrated. Most of the progeny are like
2 'London Sweetheart' and show blends of salmon and carmine pink. Among the seedlings was
4 'London Sunshine' which was quite unexpected since no yellow could be seen in either parent, and yellow is rare in epiphyllums. Moreover, the parents are scentless but half the seedlings including 'London Sweetheart' and 'London Sunshine', are scented
5 *Rhipsalidopsis rosea* 'Electra' has pendent pink flowers, produced from the areoles at the ends of the joints
6 *Zygocactus truncatus,* the Christmas cactus, is easy to grow and produces cerise-red flowers in winter
7, 8, 9 Hybrid hippeastrums
10 Hippeastrum 'Picotee' a pale cream with a green throat

Zygocactus can be grafted onto a tall stock to make an umbrella-shaped specimen

Epiphyllum cuttings are easily obtained from young shoots. Even a section will make roots if the cut part is first allowed to dry. Root them in sharp sand

7

8

5

9

6

10

They need similar care.

For zygocactus . . .

Repot every two years or when the plant becomes too large for its pot, repotting when flowering has ceased. In winter maintain a minimum temperature of 50°F (10°C), increasing this to 60°F (16°C) as buds form. Water when the soil has almost dried out, throughout the winter. In June plants may be placed out of doors in semi-shade. Plants do not like a sunny position in an unshaded greenhouse; they do better in a medium-lighted room in the house. Give them a weak liquid feed after flowering. When plants are in bud do not move them and at this time, in particular, protect them from draughts. The causes of bud drop are too wet or too dry a soil or a changeable atmosphere. Propagation is by cuttings which are best taken in early summer and rooted in sharp sand, spraying them occasionally. Or plants may be grafted on to *Pereskie* stock.

Growing a plant until it produces a wonderful flower brings a great sense of achievement. Hippeastrums are tremendously rewarding in this respect.

Hippeastrum (hip-pe-as-trum)

A genus of S. American, greenhouse, bulbous plants often referred to as *Amaryllis*, to which they are closely related. The large, showy, trumpet flowers of the hybrids, ranging in colour from the richest velvety crimson to the more delicate shades of pink and white, also bi-coloured, rank them among the most prized of winter and spring flowering pot plants for the greenhouse. Most of the hippeastrums offered in trade lists are of hybrid origin.

Cultivation Pot new bulbs in January, choosing a pot size to leave no more than ¾ inch width of soil between the bulb and the pot rim. Bulbs should be planted to half their depth only, in John Innes No 2 compost, or a mixture of 2 parts of turfy loam, and 1 part of sharp sand, plus a double handful of bonemeal to each bushel of the mixture. Start them into growth in a temperature of 60°F (16°C) and give no water for the first two weeks, then start with small amounts. As flower spikes appear, within about 3 weeks of being started, the temperature can rise to 65–70°F (18–21°C) by day, with a night minimum of 60°F (16°C). Keep the plants well watered and fed with liquid manure while growing, syringeing twice daily and maintaining a humid atmosphere. Remove dead flower heads if seed is not required. Gradually reduce the water supply from July to September (according to the time the bulbs were started into growth) until the pots are stored dry in a minimum

temperature of 40°F (4°C) for winter. Examine and repot as necessary in January, removing all dead roots. Renew the surface compost of bulbs not repotted, and start them into growth.

Young plants raised from seed should not be dried off for the winter until after their first flowering, but will need less water while the older bulbs are resting. Sow seed as soon as it is ripe, in a temperature of 60–65°F (16–18°C). Grow on in quantities in large pots or boxes until plants are about 6 inches tall, then pot them individually into 4-inch pots for their first flowering.

Saintpaulia (pronounced in England as written, but san-pole-ee-er elsewhere) or African violets are great favourites with many women.

The plants flower practically without stopping in the greenhouse and about three times a year in dwelling rooms.

Cultivation The plants like a light soil mixture and that generally used is composed of 3 parts of peat, 1 part of loam and 1 part of sharp sand. The plants could be expected to do well in soilless composts. Saintpaulias have a small root system only and rarely require to go beyond a 5-inch pot. For this plant plastic pots have been found to be more satisfactory than clay pots. The other requisites for the plants are shade, warmth and a moist atmosphere. This latter is not easy to provide in dwellings and it is best either to stand the pot on pebbles, which are standing in water in such a way that the base of the pot is clear of the water, but so that the vapour can ascend round the plant as the water evaporates, or to plunge the pot in another container, filling the interstices with some water-retentive medium such as peat, moss, sand or vermiculite. This is kept moist at all times. The plants themselves do not take great quantities of water, but this should always be given at the same temperature. The best temperature appears to be 60°F (16°C) but provided

1 **Leaf cuttings from a Saintpaulia**
2 **Use a small pot and sandy compost**
3 **and 4 The cutting and new shoot**
5 **A selection of pelargoniums.**
Top. Left to right 'Verona',
'A Happy Thought', 'Distinction'.
Centre, left to right 'Mrs Parker',
'Henry Cox', 'Wilhelm Ian Guth',
'Marechal Macmahon'. *Below,
left to right* 'Mrs Mappin',
'Harry Hieover', 'Flower of Spring'
'Black Douglas'

If you have named or selected forms of hippeastrum these can be increased by offsets removed and potted separately when the plants are inspected in January

You get better plants ultimately if you prevent young saintpaulias from flowering. Pick off the buds until the plant reaches a good size

it is not too cold or too warm, the exact temperature does not seem to matter as much as seeing that this temperature is always maintained. Waterings where the temperature fluctuates will cause the appearance of unsightly white blotches on the leaves. The temperature should ideally be 55°F (13°C) at night, and 70°F (21°C) during the daytime, and if this can be kept going throughout the year the plants will do particularly well. However, this is not always possible and lower readings will slow down growth, but will not cause any damage, provided that the temperature does not fall for long below 50°F (10°C). When temperatures are low the soil should be kept rather dry and the atmosphere should also not be too moist. Established plants should be given weak feeds at fortnightly intervals between April and October. Between November and mid-February no shading is necessary, but after this date the sun may get rather fierce and light shading should be supplied which will require intensifying at the end of April. This is a good time for doing any potting on that may be necessary.

There must be more **pelargoniums** grown on windowsills than any other plant. And there is such a wonderful variety. You can have many colours in the zonal types (these also have banded leaves from which they take their name), ornamental leaves with many variegations, scented leaves, double and single flowers and the pansy-faced kinds or regal pelargoniums.

Cultivation In general pelargoniums grown in pots will do well in the John Innes potting composts, though it is advisable to add a little extra lime to neutralise the acidity of the peat. Alternatively, particularly for potting on rooted cuttings, a suitable soil mixture consists of 2 parts of good loam, 1 part of sand, 1 part of peat, all parts by bulk, not weight, plus 1 pint of charcoal and 1 cupful of ground limestone per bushel of the mixture. The ingredients should be throughly mixed together and then watered with a liquid fertiliser with a high potash content. Some growers have been successful with the 'no-soil' composts (peat/sand mixtures plus balanced fertilisers), while others use ordinary good garden soil which has been cleared of worms and sterilised to kill harmful soil organisms.

Pelargoniums should never be overpotted. When repotting becomes necessary it is often possible, by removing old compost and slightly reducing the size of the root-ball, to repot into pots of the same size; otherwise the plants should be moved into pots one size larger only. They should always be potted firmly.

Although plants should be watered freely during the growing period, in spring and summer, they should never be overwatered and, in any case, the pots in which they are grown should be properly crocked and the soil mixture should be free-draining so that surplus moisture can get away quickly, otherwise various root-rots and stem-rots may be encouraged. In winter plants will need little water, though the soil in the pots should not be allowed to dry out.

To keep plants growing freely and to maintain good leaf colour it is necessary to feed them during the growing season. Regular weak applications of proprietary liquid fertiliser should be given from about a month after the plants are in their final pots, until September. It should be noted, however, that plants in the fancy-leaved group should either not be fed at all, or the feed they are given should not contain nitrogen. These kinds should, in any case, be given less water than others.

A number of zonal varieties can be induced to flower in winter, when blooms are always welcome. The method is to take cuttings in the spring, by normal propagation methods described below. The young plants are grown on steadily during the summer and all flower buds are removed until late September. Plants treated in this way should flower throughout the winter months. It is best to maintain a minimum temperature of 60°F (16°C) and the plants should be given as much light as possible. During the summer the plants may be placed in a sunny cold frame or the pots may be plunged in a sunny, sheltered place out of doors. They should be brought into

1 *Saintpaulia ionantha* has cultivars in a wide variety of flower colours. The white ones are the most unusual
2 *Vallota speciosa,* a bulbous plant from South Africa, has funnel-shaped, scarlet red flowers
3 This hippeastrum is a typical example of a bicoloured flower in which two contrasting colours appear in the bloom
4 Pelargonium 'Carisbrooke' has soft rose-pink petals with darker markings
5 The white flowers of pelargonium 'Muriel Harris' are feathered with red
6 Pelargonium 'Black Prince'

the greenhouse in September.

Propagation of regal pelargoniums is by cuttings, which, like those of the other types, root easily. They should be about 3 inches long, taken from the top of the lateral shoots. They are trimmed back to a node and the bottom leaves are removed. They will root quickly in a sterile rooting compost, in pots or in a propagating frame in the greenhouse. Bottom heat is not required. Cuttings of this type are usually taken in July or August.

Plants which are to be used for summer bedding purposes are raised from cuttings taken in August or September, rooting several in each 5-inch pot, or in boxes, spacing the cuttings 2 inches apart. In February the rooted cuttings are potted into individual 3-inch pots and kept in a temperature of 45–50°F (7–10°C) until April. They are then hardened off in a cold frame before planting them out of doors in late May or early June, when all danger of frost is over. Do not plant shallowly; it is best to take out a hole large enough and deep enough to take the plant up to its first pair of leaves. Leggy plants may be planted more deeply. Remove dead leaves and flowers as soon as they are seen and pinch out long, unwanted shoots from time to time to keep the plants bushy. Keep the

True geraniums are the hardy herbaceous summer-flowering plants which we grow in our rock gardens and borders. Pelargoniums are only hardy in very sheltered districts

Leaves of the scented species of pelargoniums when added to sponge cakes and fruit jellies gives them distinctive flavours

plants well watered in dry weather. A gentle overhead spray in the evenings in hot weather is beneficial. In September, before the first frosts, the plants should be lifted and brought into the greenhouse for the winter. The shoots should be cut back, long roots trimmed and the plants potted into small pots. The minimum winter temperature in the greenhouse should be around 42°F (5°C).

There is a pretty plant you often see in cottage windows.

Vallota (val-lo-ta)

A genus of one species, a bulbous plant from Cape Province, South Africa, where it is known as the George lily, but in Britain as Scarborough lily, after some bulbs were washed ashore there from a shipwreck. It is not reliably hardy in Britain, but is an admirable pot plant for a sunny window-sill. *V. speciosa* (syn. *V. purpurea*) reaches 1–2 feet, and has broad leaves, to 18 inches long and erect stems bearing up to 10 large, funnel-shaped, glowing scarlet-red flowers in August and September; there is a white variety, *alba,* and other varieties have been recorded.

Cultivation The bulbs are best potted in July in a compost of equal parts of fibrous loam, leafmould and sharp sand. The tip of the large bulb should be just below the surface and potted firmly. Do not repot for several years, but give regular feeds with liquid fertilisers while the bulbs are growing, before flowering. Ample water is required during the growing season, but the soil should be kept nearly dry while the plants are dormant, after the leaves die down. Propagation is by offsets removed when repotting.

Offset

This is a term commonly used for a young plant which can be detached from the parent plant and thus forms an easy means of propagation.

Leaf cuttings Healthy, well-developed leaves of numerous plants provide a useful means of propagation. Those that root particularly easily by this means include various begonias, such as *Begonia rex,* gloxinias, saintpaulias, streptocarpus, and some ferns, both tender and hardy. After removing a leaf from the parent plant make a few light incisions with a sharp knife across the veins on the underside and then lay the leaf on the surface of moist compost, consisting of peat and sharp sand. Peg the leaf down gently; hairpins are useful for this purpose. Leaf cuttings should be shaded from direct sunlight and have a reasonably warm and moist atmosphere. Begonia leaves, among others, will produce roots quite quickly, even when just placed in a saucer of water.

4

5

6

CHAPTER FIFTEEN
HOUSE PLANTS

The type of heating that you use and the temperatures you maintain in your various rooms during the winter will affect the types of plant you can grow. Some plants, notably begonias, are very intolerant of gas fumes, so that if your rooms are heated by gas, you will not be able to grow begonias satisfactorily. If you have really warm rooms, maintaining, perhaps, an average temperature of 70°F (21°C), they will be far too warm for such plants as ivy or × *Fatshedera lizei*. With high temperatures such as these, the plants will continue growing during the winter and more water will be required. The winter growth may not be very ornamental, as the lack of light will prevent the formation of good sized leaves.

In any natural climate the highest temperatures are around midday, but many sitting rooms are kept cold during the day, when people are out at work, warm in the evening, when everyone is at home, but cool off during the late evening and the early morning after people have gone to bed.

Such a contradiction of natural rhythm is sufficient to disturb any plant and it is easy to see that keeping plants in good condition in the winter is less simple in the house than in a greenhouse. If you have some system of regular central heating, the problem is comparatively simple, but for rooms with only sporadic warmth, the matter is less straightforward. However, there are house plants to suit all conditions.

It is fairly safe to say that no plant will tolerate the conditions that are to be found on a mantelpiece above a coal fire. The atmosphere is far too dry and the alternations of cold and roasting heat are too much for all plants, except the toughest succulents. Even if the temperature is equable, plants that are put too near the window risk being chilled, or even frosted, when the weather is very cold and they should be moved further into the room during these periods.

Even when the temperature is satisfactory, the dry atmosphere that we like in our rooms is not beneficial to plants. This, however, can easily be overcome, by placing the pots in a larger container and filling this container with some moisture-retentive material. Peat is most frequently used, but moss or mica powder does equally well. Some people get perfectly satisfactory results with damp newspaper, which is topped with moss to look more elegant. By these means we can maintain a moist atmosphere in the immediate surroundings of the plant without either affecting the atmosphere of our rooms or the correct

Variegated plants can be perpetuated only by vegetative propagation, by rooting cuttings or taking layers

Invest in a thermometer so that you know the average temperature of your rooms and choose your house plants accordingly

1 The lavender-blue flowers and persistent pink bracts of *Aechmea rhodocyanea,* a tough house plant
2 *Maranta mackoyana* must be protected from sunlight to keep its leaf colour
3 *Ficus elastica variegata,* the Indiarubber Plant, a good room plant, it also valuable for greenhouse decoration
4 A *Philodendron scandens*

state of moisture of the soil ball.

More house plants are killed by over watering than by any other cause. Like human beings, plants cannot live without water, but, again like human beings, they can be drowned. However, this analogy cannot be pressed too far. Human beings need water at regular intervals, but plants need water most when they are making growth. This is usually during the spring and summer.

When to give water is only satisfactorily learned by experience, but the following hard and fast rules are generally acceptable.
1 When water is applied, it should be in sufficient quantity to moisten the whole of the soil ball. The water should be at room temperature. Rain water is preferable but not essential.

1 A group of flowering house plants all of which add colour indoors in winter
2 The arrow-shaped leaves of *Philodendron hastatum* need frequent cleaning
3 The Rugby Football Plant, or Water Melon Plant, *peperomia sandersii*
4 A collection of house plants which includes (*Back left to right*) *hedera canariensis, ficus elastica,* sansevieria. (*Front, left to right*) croton, dieffenbachia, *begonia masoniana,* maranta, peperomia and aphelandra

2 The soil should be allowed to dry out between waterings. This is not too easy to interpret. We do not want the soil to become dust dry, but on the other hand, we want to avoid saturation. A useful rule of thumb with clay pots and soil mixtures, is to strike the side of the pot with your knuckle. If the resultant sound is dull, watering is not needed, but if it is a ringing sound, water should be applied. With peat mixtures the weight of the pot is a more reliable indication. If it feels light, water is wanted, but not if it feels heavy. The same applies, but to a lesser extent, with soil mixtures in plastic pots. These are much the most difficult to gauge.

3 During cold weather plants make little or no growth and so require little water. Growth is also slowed down when there is little light. It is safe, therefore, during the winter to keep all watering down to a minimum, even though the room may be kept at quite a high temperature. Naturally plants in warm rooms will require more than those in cool surroundings.

4 From about mid-April it is probable that growth will start and so more water may be required. Be cautious, nevertheless, un-

If a plant is making new leaves and stems it is almost certain also to be making new roots

If the soil is too wet the roots cannot breathe and will rot unless the soil dries out quickly

4

til you see new leaves appearing. It is possible to knock the plant out of its pot to see if new roots (characterised by their white tips) are forming and to replace the soil ball without disturbance. When growth is vigorous water will be needed more frequently. 'Stopping' checks growth temporarily and watering should be on a reduced scale until a resumption of growth is seen.

5 By the end of August it is advisable to discourage much further growth and encourage the plant to ripen its new growth. This is done by keeping the plant as dry as possible.

6 The type of leaf will give some indication of the plant's requirements. Plants with thick leaves or with succulent leaves (such as the large-leaved ficus and sansevieria) can tolerate longer periods without water than thin-leaved plants. These latter will

Dusty leaves inhibit growth. Clean them often with a soft tissue and clean rain water

The leaves of bromeliads such as aechmea and neoregelia form a 'vase'. Water these plants by keeping this filled with water, preferably rain, to keep deposits from forming on the leaves

probably wilt when they become too dry and they should be watered at once. The thicker leaved plants will not wilt and so should be inspected frequently. Drought, unless acute, will not kill them but may cause subsequent leaf drop.

If leaves turn yellow and fall off, it usually indicates over-watering. However some plants, such as *Ficus benjamina,* will

naturally shed their year-old leaves in the autumn and most plants shed a few leaves in the course of the year. Excessive defoliation is almost certainly due to incorrect watering; although it can be caused by under-watering as well as by over watering. If the plant becomes unsteady in the pot, this is generally due to root-rot caused by excessive water and is

very difficult to arrest. Some leaves will wilt in the summer if they are in direct hot sunlight. If the soil appears to be satisfactorily moist, a syringeing of the leaves with water will generally restore them to their normal turgidity, and in any case, they will resume their normal appearance as soon as the sunlight goes.

During the summer, when growth is most vigorous, the plants may be fed. A liquid feed is most easily applied and should be given according to the instructions on the bottle. Little and often is invariably better than doses in excess of those recommended. Unless the plant is really well-rooted, feeding should not be applied and is not necessary for plants that have been repotted. Repotting is done in

1 *Hedera helix* 'Chicago', a pointed-leaved ivy with (*front*) *Chlorophytum capense,* sometimes known as the Spider Plant
2 The poinsettia, *Euphorbia pulcherrima,* a flamboyant plant for winter flowers
3 A young plant of *Tetrastigma voineriana*
4 *Sansevieria trifasciata laurentii,* and hedera 'Heiss' in the foreground
5 *Scindapsus aureus,* the Devil's Ivy
6 The deeply-cut leaves of *Philodendron elegans* are an attractive addition to any collection of indoor plants

4   5   6

the early summer. For the majority of house plants the John Innes potting compost No 2 is the best. Plants are usually potted on into a pot one size larger. Plants from 5-inch pots are put into 6-inch pots and so on. The only exception is that the 4-inch pot is very rarely used and plants are moved from 3-inch to 5-inch pots. Plants with very thin roots such as begonias and peperomias do better in a mixture of 2 parts of leafmould to 1 part of

sharp sand, while epiphytes, such as the bromeliads, are usually given a mixture of peat, leafmould and sharp sand. However, it is only rarely that epiphytes require any potting on, as they use the soil as an anchorage only. After being potted on the plants should be kept on the dry side until the roots have penetrated the new soil. It is best to move plants from 2-inch pots to 5-inch pots after a year, as the 3-inch pots dry out so quickly, but after that most house plants will need repotting only every other year. Thr second year the plant will will need feeding.

1 *Sansevieria trifasciata laurentii,* or Mother-in-law's Tongue
2 A collection of ferns in a bark container, with helxine added in

the front
3 *Dracaena godseffiana* has opposite leaves heavily spotted with cream and likes a warm room with plenty of light
4 The striped dracaena produces whorls of green leaves, edged and heavily marked with cream
5 A poisonous plant *Dieffenbachia amoena,* justifiably called Dumb Cane
6 *Dracaena massangeana,* a spreading plant with variegated leaves
7 Evergreen plants grown for indoor decoration provide interest all the year round.Many have attractive leaves like this *Fittonia argyroneura*

1

2

3

4

Climbing aeroids like philodendron, syngonium and scindapsus will grow more luxuriantly if they are encouraged to climb a 'pole' made of wire netting stuffed with damp moss

Remember the darker the green and the thicker the leaf the more tolerant the plant will be of shady conditions. You can grow these plants away from the window

5

6

7

CHAPTER SIXTEEN
BOTTLE GARDENS

Once you have grown house plants inside a bottle you will always be enchanted with this form of captive gardening. My own bottle gardens consist of two carboys, two outsize brandy balloons and an outsize storage jar. But I have made them in many other vessels. Naturally the wider the mouth of the bottle the easier it is to plant it, but if it is very wide you may need a lid or stopper.

The success of this type of gardening depends on the creation of an isolated microclimate inside the vessel and on giving it plenty of light.

Most leafy plants from warm countries need, in cultivation, not only heat but air humidity. This vital component of growth —not to be confused with soil moisture— is the most difficult for the amateur to understand, because it is invisible and not readily discernible, while the instrument which measures its concentration—the hygrometer—is not a standard piece of equipment.

In a greenhouse, air moisture is provided by 'damping down' the floor, staging, or both. But when we come to cultivate these plants in rooms, air dryness becomes a serious problem, because all our methods of room heating tend to dry out the air excessively.

To enclose room plants within glass was a logical step, and from 1840 or so until 1900, Wardian Cases—so-called after their originator, Dr Nathaniel Ward—were a feature of many Victorian homes.

Wardian case
Nathaniel Ward (1791–1868) a London doctor and naturalist, accidentally discovered the plant-growing case named after him. Wishing to study a chrysalis he brought back from the countryside he buried it in some soil in an almost airtight glass jar. He noticed that seeds in the soil soon began to germinate, forming plants which grew vigorously. He continued making experiments and in 1838 he made the first Wardian case from metal and glass. It was soon used to make fern-cases in which moisture-loving ferns could be grown indoors inside the case in spite of a dry surrounding atmosphere. It also enabled living plants to be dispatched successfully over long distances when transport was slow and often difficult. It was used by Robert Fortune when he made his plant-collecting expedition to China in 1845. Later, it made possible the introduction of tea plants to India, the world-wide distribution of quinine-producing plants and the first cultivation of bananas outside China.

Apart from such practical uses, the Wardian Case became unfashionable early

in this century and few remain in existence. During the 1940s, in the U.S.A., the same principle was applied to an indoor gardener's 'gimmick'—growing plants in a bottle. This was introduced to Britain about 1956 and is now so popular that planted bottles are sold commercially.

The standard bottle for gardening is the large, round, 10 gallon carboy, which until recently was used for acid and distilled water (now they are being replaced by plastic containers). Oval carboys and the vertical-sided demijohn used for spirits are also attractive. In fact any bottle can be used as long as its aperture is large enough to allow plants to be inserted.

Bottling plants is much easier than the final result may lead one to imagine— certainly simpler than putting a ship in a

bottle! After cleaning the carboy thoroughly an inch-deep layer of small crocks inserted. This is followed by soil, which can be poured in through a paper funnel or a cardboard tube to avoid soiling the glass. A good mixture consists of 1 part of fibrous loam, 2 parts of peat and 1 part of coarse sand, or 2 parts of John Innes No. 1 potting compost and 1 part of extra peat can be mixed. The soil mixture should be just damp, by no means wet, and the soil layer should be 5–6 inches deep.

The only tools needed are a cane with a cotton reel pushed firmly on to one end and a length of 1 inch wide wooden lath, pointed at one end. Small plastic tools, a 'spade' at one end, a 'fork' or 'rake' at the other, are sold for use by indoor gardeners. If these are cut in half and the

1

cut-ends pushed into lengths of cane, two useful tools can be made for use when the bottle is being prepared and planted. With the cotton reel the soil is firmed down; the flat end of the lath is used to push the soil about and the pointed end to excavate planting holes. It is essential to make each hole large enough to accommodate the roots of the plant destined for it. It may be necessary to take some soil off the root ball before it can be passed through the neck of the bottle.

Start with the plants round the outside of the bottle (to avoid dropping soil on those already planted). Push the root ball through the aperture, then hold the plant by its leaves, push it gently through, and let it drop. It can then be pushed into its hole with the cane and lath (or with the plastic tools), the roots covered with soil, and the cotton reel used to make the plant firm.

Little attention is needed once the bottle garden is planted. If the top is kept on, little or no water is needed (plants have been known to flourish in bottle gardens for several years with no extra water added from the time of planting), but condensation will form on the glass at certain times; this gradually clears as the moisture runs down the inside of the glass into the soil. This is, in fact, a continual cycle; water given off through the leaves of the plants in the form of vapour, condenses on the glass, runs back into the soil, is absorbed again through the roots of the plants and is again given off through the foliage. If the bottle is open a cupful of water every month or so in summer is desirable. Dead leaves are removed by cutting them off with a piece of razor-blade wired to a cane; they can then be lifted out on a pointed cane. Keep the bottle out of direct sunlight, but make sure that it is in good indirect light.

Exactly the same principles, but less trouble, can be used if it is desired to plant a large goldfish bowl, a brandy glass, a wide-necked jar.

Plants should be purchased in the smallest pots available. One large firm specializing in house plants, supplies small specimens intended for use in bottle gardens. Suitable plants are: *Calathea oppenheimiana, C. ornata, C. zebrina; Cryptanthus bivittatus, C. tricolor* and others; *Fittonia argyroneura, F. verschaffeltii; Maranta leuconeura kerchoveana, M. massangeana, M. makoyana; Neanthe bella; Peperomia magnoliaefolia, P. caperata, P. hederaefolia, P. sandersii* and others; *Vriesia splendens.* Ferns such as *Asplenium nidus* and *Pellaea rotundifolia* are suitable. Rampant growers such as tradescantia must be avoided, and flowering plants are more trouble than they are worth.

In one of my wide necked jars I have sloped the soil, arranged an attractive piece of rock on the summit and planted **Nertera** which now covers the soil. This is a charming little plant. There is one species only in common cultivation, *N. granadensis* (syn. *N. depressa*). It is a low-growing, spreading plant, its main decorative feature being its dense crop of bright orange, pea-sized berries. Coming from New Zealand, Australia and South America, it is almost hardy in Britain and is sometimes grown permanently on rock gardens, with winter protection.

Cultivation *N. granadensis* is normally grown as a greenhouse pot plant, in sandy compost, such as 2 parts of sandy loam, 1 part each of sand and leafmould. Plants should be shaded from strong sunlight. Pot in spring in warmth and afterwards, when the plants are established, move the pots to a cool place to assist flower and berry formation. Keep the plants well watered. Out of doors they may be grown on shady parts of the rock garden in ordinary light rich soil, but will need some protection in winter. They are easily raised from seed sown in warmth in spring or may be increased by potting small pieces separated from established plants.

One of my carboys contains ferns and these look extremely attractive seen through glass. Most women like ferns, but usually the atmosphere in a home is too dry for them. A bottle garden suits them well and you can find many pretty little species. You may have some from which you can propagate.

For bottle gardens lower the ferns into place when they are quite tiny. You will find it easy to prick them into the soil.

Propagation In spring when the ferns are repotted and just as new growth begins to swell, a plant can be divided and the divisions potted up separately and kept close until growth is evident.

Some ferns, for example Aspidium (shield fern), occasionally produce small plants on the fronds. These can be pegged down into pots or boxes of fine compost and severed after rooting has taken place.

The most interesting method of propagation is by sowing the spores that are produced in the spore cases (sporangia) on the backs of the fronds. Put a mature frond into a white envelope for a few days to dry off, and collect the powdery spores. Sow these on the surface of sandy compost, previously sterilised, in a pan first half filled with crocks. Stand the pan in shallow water, cover it with glass or polythene and shade. Autumn sowing is best but the spores may be saved until the spring. The resulting green plant, or prothallus, bears no resemblance to the original fern but is the sexual generation in the life cycle of the fern. The prothalli should be put into a pan or box about an inch apart, just pressed on to the soil, and the resulting tiny fern plants potted up individually once they are big enough to handle.

I use cryptanthus to give contrast of textures. These can be first arranged on a piece of cork if you wish to give height to the arrangement of plants. Fix them in position with an elastic band and lower into place.

Cryptanthus (krip-tan-thus)
Sometimes called 'earth stars' an allusion to their starfish-like shapes. A small genus of dwarf, tufted, spiny plants from Brazil, suitable for the stovehouse or as house plants. The flowers are mostly white, and borne in a dense tuft of bracts in the centre of the rosette.

Stolons are produced in the outer leaf axils, making offsets which can be removed for propagation. When grown as house plants they should be kept dry or nearly dry in winter. In the house they need a light position; the smaller kinds are suitable for growing in bottle gardens.

2

1 A variety of plants lend themselves to being grown in a bottle garden and they need little attention after they have been planted. Small specimens can be bought for this purpose
2 A nineteenth-century example of a Wardian case, from which the bottle garden developed

CHAPTER SEVENTEEN
FLOWER ARRANGEMENT

Flower arrangement

Floral decorations are made or should be designed to suit their surroundings and although an oriental-styled arrangement might well suit a living room or, if it is designed on a large scale, the more spacious class room and conference hall it is generally not so suited to large or more ornate interiors. Here, most of the flowers have to compete with coloured, even patterned furnishings and walls and so it follows that to be noticeable the arrangements must be large as well as colourful.

In general, there are two great divisions of styles; one in which the accent is on line, silhouette and/or design and the other in which colour is the dominant feature and in which the mass tends to be set inside a certain outline. Again in general these tend to be either Oriental or Occidental in origin.

Modern schools But since flower arrangement is such a personal art it is also fluid and ever-changing and so we have many variations on these two themes. At times the two are joined and we see a contemporary style which is an amalgam of line and mass.

What is a flower? Universally, the term 'flower arrangement' is more comprehensive than at first might appear. By 'flower' we mean any type of plant material and, paradoxical though it may be, many an arrangement is made without a true flower as part of it. Obviously, leaves and

2

3

1

4

Cut the firm edge away from wire netting. It will then be more malleable

To fix candles on pinholders first warm the pinholder. Use the same method to remove the candle again

5

6

7

branches, blossom and berries form a part of many flower arrangements as one would expect, but perhaps not so obviously, so do bare branches, driftwood, stems, roots, seed pods, grasses and all kinds of fruiting parts of plants as well as fungi, lichens, mosses and even seaweeds.

Containers to use The same liberal attitude is adopted by the modern flower arranger towards containers. For centuries flower vases have tended to be things apart, vessels designed only to support and display flowers. But for the modern imaginative flower arranger, anything goes—so long as it can be made to hold water or some water-retentive material and is suitable for the flowers, setting and occasion.

There are exceptions, of course. For example, period arrangements ought to be made not only in the style known to be fashionable at the time in question but also in vessels of the period. Alternatively, faithful reproductions can be used. Unless

this is done one never captures the true flavour of the period. They ought also, and for the same reason, to contain flowers grown and known at the same time.

Japanese flower arrangement Centuries ago, the Japanese devised sophisticated ways of anchoring stems which meant that the old, massed Rikkwa style was dropped in favour of arrangements in which stems could be held just as the arranger required. These then became more and more stylised. As they were originally linked with religion in some form or another—as indeed flowers were in all parts of the world—Japanese flower arrangement continued down through the

1 A bottle is used for long-lasting arrangement of achillea, rushes, yucca seed heads and mahonia leaves. Gourds are wired into place
2 Chicken netting, either

galvanised or plastic covered is crushed to form a base of any shape or size. Absorbent white Florapak or green Oasis hold stems firmly and keep blooms fresh. Pin holders held by Plasticine fit firmly in the bottom of containers
3 A white arrangement for the centre of a table. The first central stem is put in vertically to define the height and is the pivot from which the stems will appear to radiate
4 The side stems of stocks determine the width of the arrangement, and intermediate stems are neither higher nor longer than the first stems
5 Some of the larger flowers, viburnum, should be recessed to hide the holder as well as to provide depth and interest to the contour
6 The rose buds, which will open wide, are added last, to the heart of the arrangement. The whole arrangement provides a delightful effect for the centre of a table
7 Beech leaves and chrysanthemums

1

2

centuries to be linked with religious symbolism or spiritual interpretations.

The three main stems were given greatest importance and were shown to signify Heaven, Man and Earth. But this attitude should not deter the severely practical minded because the proportions of these stems are of such practical and logical beauty that they can be followed easily and with pleasing results. Furthermore, the mystical Japanese flower arrangement once said to be possible to execute only after a long period of contemplation and even meditation, has now been digested and revised in the form of Ikebana, possibly the most universally popular form of simple flower arrangement at this time.

Patterns for designs Because the materials used are so diverse, it is unlikely that one would ever see a flower arrangement exactly like another, but it is possible to see many that look alike and are made in the same style or pattern. This is mainly

because it is the purpose of flower arrangement to display each flower to advantage and we find that a certain number of stems tend to fall into certain styles, mainly pyramidal or conical—even if a definite pattern was not the original intention. This is particularly the case when uniform flowers have to be arranged.

Choice of containers Although beauty is the goal, one's aim should be practical also. Flower arrangements not only need to suit their surroundings but also their containers, so that vessel and contents make a unit. Flowers which are long stemmed and heavy need anchoring well. In a container which is too small for them they may overbalance. Some flowers absorb more water than others and so need a deep vessel. Choice of container is vitally important. Not only must it hold the flowers well but it needs also to match the mood, suit the colour, texture and style of the contents.

Keeping flowers fresh Since flowers are gathered and brought indoors to enjoy, it follows that they should be kept alive as long as possible. Contrary to common belief, flowers should not be taken from their vases each day to have a piece of stem cut away. Neither should the water be changed each day if proper precautions are taken, although the level should be kept topped up, in case the water evaporates to danger level. This understood, it follows that once a flower arrangement is made it should remain decorative for many days.

The most important factor for lasting freshness is that all materials should be hardened properly. All should be turgid and taking water properly before arrangement. This means that as soon as possible after they are gathered, stems should be stood in deep water, covering any foliage on the stems should this be present, for at least an hour, longer if possible. By cover-

Like most of their kind lilies can be cut and arranged while the buds are just coloured. They will then open slowly in water

Blossom will take water much more easily if most of the foliage is first removed

1 and 2 An example of Ikebana. The longest stem symbolises Heaven. The second longest represents Man, linking Heaven and Earth, the shortest stem
3 Another arrangement. The central spray of *Viburnum opulus* is arranged to form the skeleton
4 A third-dimensional effect is added by the low stems in front
5 The final arrangement with alstroemerias, carnations and euphorbia

ing the leaves with water in this way, respiration is prevented and the stem will become turgid more quickly than if it had been allowed to function naturally.

To ensure quick intake of water, all but hollow and very fleshy stems should be split at the base upwards for a half inch or more according to the length of stem. This exposes the soft inner tissues. It also expels any air present which tends to cause a lock in the stem tissues and prevents water being drawn up. To prevent flowers from wilting inexplicably, as some do after arrangement even though they have had a long deep drink beforehand, it is advisable that the water into which they are stood for the preliminary drink should be heated to 70°F (21°C). Rain water is best.

Hardening and preparing materials
For a variety of reasons, some plant material once cut from the plant cannot take water easily; acacia or mimosa, apparently not at all. Only humidity round

95

the flowers and leaves keeps them fresh. You can, for instance, keep mimosa fluffy for days, even weeks, if you place it under a glass dome.

Those stems which exude a milky juice or latex, for example euphorbias, cannot take water until the juice coagulates. The easiest way to effect this is to singe the stem ends over a flame as soon as possible after cutting. Any stems which are shortened for arrangement after the singed stems have been given a deep drink should be re-singed.

Any flower which fails to become turgid, hollyhocks are examples, and all young and immature foliage, whether individual leaves or branches should have their stem ends stood in an inch or two of boiling water until turgid. The stem ends thus treated often become blackened and sometimes soft. Once it has become turgid, this portion may be cut away and if the stem has to be shortened for arrangement there should be no need to treat the new cut end.

Preservatives and nutrients Certain preservatives and nutrients help to maintain freshness. There are several proprietary brands on sale most of which contain some glucose which seems to be appreciated by most flowers. Use one level teaspoonful of glucose, sugar or one saltspoonful of honey to a pint of water.

In arrangements of fresh shrub and tree materials, especially those such as blossom in bud or Christmas evergreens which are expected to stand for some weeks, use a little of any good soluble plant food, sufficient to make a very weak solution.

There is some validity in the use of a copper coin or an aspirin tablet in the water within a container. These discourage or delay bacterial action. There is also less bacterial activity in metal containers. On the other hand, water in glass containers, especially if these are stood in sunlight, tends to become lively very rapidly.

Foul water will kill flowers or else discolour them. Always strip the leaves from the portion of stem which is to remain under water and avoid hammering or crushing woody and fibrous stems. The foamed urea plastics stem holders such as Oasis and Florapak contain formaldehyde which is a form of disinfectant and so these help keep flowers fresh.

Holding stems firmly in place If flower arrangement is to be quick and easy as well as effective it must be possible for the florist to place any stem at will and to be quite confident that it is well anchored and will remain so. One of the most versatile of stem holders is large mesh, $1\frac{1}{2}$–2 inch wire-netting. It is also possible to buy plastic-covered netting in flower shops and other places. This is quite good, especially when precious vases must not be scratched, but is not quite so malleable as the common kind. Large mesh is the most malleable and will give under the pressure of a thick stem being pushed through a crumpled mass. Small mesh on the other hand, is too rigid and so prevents arrangement. It is best to use the large mesh even for small containers. Miniature arrangements, obviously need other treatment.

Most often it is best to fill the container from rim to base with a mass of crumpled netting, first cut in a piece just a fraction wider than the greatest diameter and twice the depth of the container. If the netting is

Foundations for cones and other shapes can be bought ready formed. Use them dry for dried materials

When making all-foliage arrangements look for contrasting shapes as well as textures and colours

first folded into a 'U' shape and then squashed into the container with the cut ends uppermost, some of these cut ends may then be hooked over the rim to hold the netting firm. Sometimes netting slips in highly glazed containers.

If very large or outsize arrangements are being planned it is advisable to use more wire-netting than usual and to allow this to protrude well above the rim of the vase. It will then help to support very tall stems.

Arrangement is always easier when the netting fills the container from rim to base because then the bases of long stems are firmly held. However, this is unsightly when glass containers are used. In this case a small crumpled piece of netting should be fixed in the mouth of the container so that the stems will pass through it into the water. Low hanging materials will hide the lower part of the netting.

Lightweight containers may be half filled with sand to weight the base, with netting arranged on top.

Excellent modern alternatives to wire netting are the water-retentive foamed urea stem-holders, such as Florapak. Because these hold, but do not spill water, they are useful for arrangements which have to be stood on polished furniture. They are also useful for arrangements which have to be transported and those to be stood out of reach where they cannot be topped up daily. These can be used either to fill the vase from rim to base or, alternatively they can be used at the base of a container with wire netting arranged at the higher level near the rim.

One great advantage is that only a small portion of stem end need be inserted into the plastic which means that comparatively short stems can be used in tall arrangements.

Other plastics, Oasis for instance, evaporate quite quickly and have to be moistened daily but their great value lies in the fact that they do not quickly disintegrate and so may safely be used ex-container — in a saucer for example. Water poured into the saucer will be taken up by capillary action.

Pin holders Known as *kenzan* in Japan, pin holders are ancient stem holders brought up to date. They come in many sizes and shapes including minute examples for miniature arrangements or for holding a single flower. They are mostly used in shallow containers, but they are also sometimes useful at the base of a tall container, especially when a tall and heavy branch is to be displayed.

These holders consist of upright pin, needle or nail points projecting from a heavy metal base. Plastic pin holders are manufactured but these will not efficiently hold all types of stems. Stems are impaled on the points, either vertically or at an angle. Woody stems are more easily arranged if they are cut on a slant.

To prevent movement the pinholder should be firmly anchored before arrangement takes place. This is simply done by making four or five small pills of plasticine which should be lightly attached to the dry base of the holder. If this is then pressed against the equally dry floor of the

1 A free-style arrangement of foliage based on the sheaf form. Vine leaves add central colour
2 A jug holds a late summer bouquet
3 Materials are mounted by short wire stems, on a shaped base of Oasis

3

1

container the pills become squashed and act as washers.

No holders of any kind should ever show after an arrangement is finished. Pin holders are easy to hide by using large flowers placed low, but not actually touching the water, or leaves, stones, shells, driftwood and other objects, all of which should harmonise with the other components of the arrangement.

1 Alliums are cut short, and the stem retained for a line arrangement
2 Smooth stones hide the pin holder in the final clean effect
3 A white cherub vase holds dried flowers, wheat and pussy willow
4 Lily 'Enchantment' in a vertical design for a modern bowl
5 Seeds heads of *Iris sibirica,* held by a pin holder, complete the arrangement
6 Leaves of the horse chestnut are a favoured subject in spring
7 Gaillardias help towards a bold effect in a well arranged vase in high summer
8 An inevitable autumn choice – the richly coloured leaves of Virginia creeper

2

3

6

7

8

4

5

CHAPTER EIGHTEEN

FOLIAGE FOR CUTTING

A flower arranger needs all kinds of foliage and individual leaves to make home decorations throughout the year.

Many of the shrubs described in earlier chapters can be cut for use. There are also many perennials which are worth growing for their handsome leaves. Some also give lovely flowers.

Begin with one of our native plants, the wild lords and ladies or cuckoo pint, *Arum maculatum,* and search nursery lists for other species to go with it.

Arum (a-rum)

It is thought that the burning taste of these plants gave them the ancient name of arum from the Arabic *ar,* fire *(Araceae).* There are hardy and half-hardy perennials in this tuberous-rooted genus, grown for their showy spathes, spadices and foliage, the true flowers being insignificant.

Hardy species cultivated *A. italicum,* $1\frac{1}{2}$ feet, creamy white spathes, leaves appear in the autumn. Forms with spotted or marbled leaves such as var. *pictum,* are more showy, *A. maculatum,* the native cuckoo-pint or lords and ladies, and many other names, 6 inches, leaves plain green or dark spotted, spathes yellowish-green and spotted with purple. *A. pictum,* 1 foot, grown for its large light green leaves, spathes white within, margined with purple.

Cultivation The hardy species will thrive in any ordinary soil and prefer a shady spot. Protect species other than the native *A. maculatum* in winter with leaves.

Hardy, floriferous and beautiful into the bargain are the bergenias.

Bergenia (ber-gen-i-a)

These hardy perennial herbaceous plants with large evergreen leaves were at one time called megasca, and were at another time included with the saxifrages. The flowers which come in early spring are showy in white, pink or red-purple, borne in large heads on long stems. The large leathery, glossy leaves are decorative, especially as in some kinds the foliage is suffused with reddish colour, in winter.

Cultivars 'Ballawley Hybrid', $1\frac{1}{2}$ feet, crimson flowers, dark purplish leaves in winter. 'Delbees', 1 foot, leaves turn red in winter, flowers rosy, March–April. 'Evening Glow', 15–18 inches, dark purple flowers, reddish-bronze foliage. 'Silberlicht', ('Silver Light'), 1 foot, flowers white flushed pink, spring. Others are available

Many leaves need hardening or preparing before they are arranged. Stand the stems in an inch of boiling water until it cools

Split all woody stems upwards for an inch or so. Stand them in tepid water, up to their leaves, for a few hours before arranging them

and more are likely to be seen in cultivation as time goes on.

Cultivation These members of the saxifrage family are in no way difficult, thriving in any soil, in sun or shade. However, to get full colour in the winter leaves (and this can be very fine), it will be necessary to give the bergenias full sun exposure; and under those conditions they will also produce their flowers somewhat earlier.

For most of the year the dainty epimedium is charmingly coloured.

Epimedium (ep-im-ee-de-um)
Decorative hardy perennials for the rock garden or wild garden. In the spring the small shield-shaped leaves are pale green with pink, rose and pale lemon tints. They become deeper green in the summer and are attractively veined; by the autumn they take on rich tints of deeper colouring. The light, arching sprays of flowers are borne in spring and early summer. There are many species in cultivation.

Cultivation Plant in the autumn or spring in sandy loam enriched with leafmould or peat. Choose a cool shady border or rock garden. They do well under trees, provided the situation is not too dry, where they retain their leaves throughout the winter. They are useful for suppressing weeds. Propagation is by division of the roots in the autumn. Many of the aromatic herbs are ideal for cutting.

Ballota (ba-lo-ta)
A genus of hardy herbaceous perennial plants or sub-shrubs which are unimportant in the garden except for two species.

Species cultivated *B. pseudodictamnus,* 2 feet, is a good, pale grey-green, woolly-leaved plant for a dry sunny spot. Its small white, purple-spotted blossoms are of no particular value in the garden picture. *B pseudodictamnus* for the sake of its foliage is worthy of some effort to provide a well-drained light soil and full sun exposure.

Ruta (roo-ta)
The only species in general cultivation in this country is *R. graveolens,* known as rue or herb of grace and grown for centuries for its medicinal properties. It makes a half-woody evergreen shrub up to 3 feet in height and width. The leaves are glaucous, 3–5 inches long and composed of many leaflets up to $\frac{1}{2}$ inch long. Deep yellow, 4-petalled flowers, about $\frac{3}{4}$ inch wide are borne from July to September. 'Jackman's Blue', 2 feet, is a most desirable compact form with deep glaucous-blue leaves against which the yellow flowers contrast effectively; var. *variegata,* $2\frac{1}{2}$ feet, has leaves bordered with white.

Cultivation Although the common rue may be confined to the herb garden, the cultivars in particular make handsome, dwarf shrubs when grown for effect in herbaceous or shrub borders. Fairly severe pruning back of mature bushes is desirable in April at least every other year, in order to maintain a compact and shapely habit. Propagation is by seed sown in the spring or, where the cultivars are concerned, by cuttings 4–6 inches long made from ripened side-shoots in late summer, rooted in a cold frame. The resultant plants may be moved to their final positions the following autumn.

Artemisia (ar-tem-ees-e-a)
A large genus, widely distributed over the world, of shrubs, sub-shrubs, herbaceous perennials and annuals, grown mainly for their dainty, aromatic foliage which is very finely cut in some species. The genus shows a great diversity of habit and leaf shape: the flowers are very small and are seldom of much account, though they are often borne in large panicles or plumes. The herb used for flavourings and tarragon vinegar is a member of this family. Most of the artemisias are sun lovers, but *A. lactiflora,* with its sprays of creamy white flowers, will grow in semi-shade and is a useful plant for the herbaceous border.

Annual species cultivated *A. sacrorum viridis,* summer fire, 4 feet, strictly a sub-shrub but grown as an annual.

Herbaceous and sub-shrubs *A. absinthium,* wormwood, $1\frac{1}{2}$ feet, flowers yellow, summer. There is a good form, 'Lambrook Silver' useful for the grey border. *A. dracunculus,* tarragon, 2 feet, whitish green. *A. gnaphalodes,* 2 feet, foliage grey-white. *A. lactiflora,* 4 feet, creamy-white flowers in lumes, late summer.

Shrubs *A. abrotanum,* 3–4 feet, the well-known old man, southernwood, or lad's love, fragrant, grey, filigree foliage. *A. arborescens,* 3 feet, silvery foliage retained throughout the year. The flowers of both these shrubs, when produced, are insignificant. They are grown for their foliage.

Cultivation Plant in autumn or spring in

1 *Arum maculatum,* **our native Lords and Ladies**
2 *Bergenia purpurascens* **bears its purplish flowers in June whereas** *Bergenia cordifolia* 3 **is one of the earliest hardy perennials to flower producing its heads of pink blooms in March**
4 *Epimedium niveum* **in flower**
5 *Epimedium versicolor,* **grown especially for its ornamental foliage**

5

4

sunny borders in ordinary soil. Propagate shrubby species by summer cuttings and herbaceous by cuttings or division. Seeds may be sown in spring of annual and herbaceous species.

The beautiful ornamental cabbage and kale are at their best during the most critical season when flowers are scarce.

The crinkled leaves are most effective when used with arrangements in a vase and the plants are also colourful and long lasting in the garden. The plants are easily raised from seeds which are obtainable as variegated silver, variegated purple and variegated mixed. Sow the seeds in April or May and transplant the seedlings about 18 inches apart. Cultivation is the same as for ordinary cabbage.

If you have shade, grow hostas.

Hosta Plaintain lily. Hardy herbaceous plants, natives of E. Asia, principally Japan, valued for their large decorative leaves in variable greens, some glaucous, some with variegated patterns in green, silver and gold. Their flower racemes carry tubular, lily-like blooms mainly in summer, in shades purple-lilac or white.

Preferring partial shade, hostas are ideal for mass planting in woodland settings or other shady places. Used in clumps they discourage weeds from establishing in border edges where they make bold contrast with taller growing plants. As moisture-loving plants they are excellent for planting by streams or on the banks of ponds. When grown in pots or tubs and watered adequately hostas are fine for use in terrace or patio gardening, or in greenhouses and conservatories. Their leaves and flowers last well in water and are used widely in floral arrangements.

Since it is important that you should get the right patterned leaf here is a list of the species.

Species cultivated *H. albo-marginata* (syn. *H. lancifolia albo-marginata*), 1 foot, leaves with a narrow white border, flowers violet. *H. crispula* (syn. *H. fortunei marginato-alba*), 2 feet, large leaves with a broad pure white border, flowers pale lilac. *H. decorata,* broad oval leaves, narrowly edged with white, flower stems to 2 feet, flowers dark violet. *H. fortunei,* 2 feet, broad glaucous green leaves, flowers pale

lilac; var. *albo-picta,* leaves yellowish-white, darkening later with a green edge. *H. lancifolia* (syn. *H. japonica*), 1½ feet, narrow, dark green leaves, flowers pale lilac. *H. plantaginea,* 1½ feet, large glossy, green leaves, flowers white, fragrant, early autumn. *H. rectifolia,* 1½ feet, leaves green, 1 foot long, flowers deep lilac, carried well above the foliage. *H. sieboldiana,* 2 feet, leaves grey-blue, flowers lilac-white, one of the most handsome species. *H. tardiflora,* 1 foot, narrow, shining green leaves, flowers lilac-mauve, late September to November. *H. undulata,* 15 inches, leaves green with a white central band, wavy edged or spirally twisted, flowers pale lilac; var. *erromena* (syns. *H. japonica fortis, H. lancifolia fortis*), 3 feet, leaves rich green, flowers dark lilac. *H. ventricosa,* 2½ feet long, heart-shaped green leaves, flowers dark lavender.

Cultivation Ground preparation should include the addition of plenty of well-decayed manure, and peat if the soil tends to dry out quickly. Mulch annually in spring with compost or manure. Plant in autumn or spring. Keep moist during dry

1 Ornamental cabbages are popular with flower arrangers
2 Hostas in variety
3 The red ornamental kale, much used in decorative floral arrangements
4 Ornamental kale, with a paler central area to the leaf

If you let seed of ornamental cabbage grow unthinned you can raise miniature 'cabbage roses' for small arrangements

Hosta leaves can be left to fade on the plant and then skeletonised. Simply leave them to soak in old rain water

spells. For pot culture, use John Innes No. 3 compost or 2 parts of loam to 1 part of decayed manure and sand mixture. Pot in March or April and overwinter in a cold frame. Hostas are easily increased by dividing clumps, preferably when new growth starts in spring. Seed is available

of some species; this should be sown in John Innes seed compost in spring under glass.

Many flower arrangers have learned to value elaeagnus.

Elaeagnus (el-e-ag-nus)

Hardy deciduous and evergreen decorative shrubs with insignificant, but fragrant, silver-coloured flowers, resembling small fuchsias.

Plant the deciduous species from October to December, and the evergreen species in April or September. All thrive in dryish, ordinary soil either in an open, but somewhat sheltered position, or against a south or west-facing wall.

Grey and silver-leaved plants. Every group of plants, from trees down to the smallest of rock plants, can supply its quota of grey and silver.

Widely used in formal bedding schemes are *Centaurea candidissima* and *C. gymnocarpa,* together with varieties of *Senecio cineraria,* the finest forms of which are 'White Diamond', 'Ramparts' and 'Hoar

Fróst'.

The centaureas are hardy perennials, the senecios sub-shrubs, but all may be treated as half-hardy annuals for bedding purposes, sowing the seed in heat in spring for planting out in late May or early June.

'White Diamond' and 'Ramparts' both have striking foliage, thickly felted with silvery-white. 'Hoar Frost' is aptly described by its name and there is a newer and more compact form, 'Dwarf Silver', with even brighter and more exciting leaf colour than the older varieties.

There are two stately silver biennials, both of which top 6 feet in height, that make plants for outstanding architectural beauty for the back of the border, either in groups or as individual plants. The Scots thistle, *Onopordon acanthium,* has leaves that bear a strong resemblance to those of the spiny acanthus, except that they are silvery-white and covered with a fine greyish patina.

This statuesque plant, which is easily raised from seed sown out-of-doors in May, has stems that are curiously ribbed and flanged and topped with striking grey thistle-heads that open to mauve-pink.

In their first season plants will make a rosette of leaves at soil level, elongating these into 6 foot flower stems the following year. Although the Scots thistle dies off after flowering, it will seed itself freely—in the manner of wild thistles—and young plants are likely to appear in unexpected corners of the garden.

This ability to seed freely is one that is shared by the second biennial—that attractive member of the mullein family that used to be known as *Verbascum broussa* and has now been re-named *V. bombyciferum.* The leaves of this plant have the appearance of having been cut out of thick flannel, they are thick and fleecy and are covered with a coarse down. During their first winter grey-white rosettes of leaves provide interest. The fall flower spikes, sometimes 12 feet in height, are clustered with butter-yellow flowers partially encased in silver-white fleece.

Grey and silver make an effective contrast in the herbaceous border where groupings of these colours can be used as buffers between others that clash, or to tone down the effect of plants whose colours are too brash or too brilliant for their surroundings. Many, like the silver-grey perennial *Anaphalis triplinervis,* also make first-rate edging plants which, in addition to being completely trouble-free, perform a valuable role as cover-and-smother plants.

This Himalayan perennial is particularly useful for the latter purpose. Plants

make compact, silver-grey hummocks whose attraction is in no way diminished when the clusters of papery, white everlasting flowers begin to appear in July.

Stachys lanata, popularly known as 'Lambs' Ears' from the appearance of its down-covered fleshy leaves, is another good cover plant for the edge of the herbaceous or mixed border. It spreads very fast—too fast, perhaps, where space is restricted—and clumps are liable to get straggly and untidy. It is advisable to lift and divide them every other year or so.

Many other grey-leaved perennials serve a dual purpose. *Veronica incana,* for example, as well as forming a silvery carpet at soil level, has delightful flower spikes of violet-blue that act as a perfect foil to the leaves. 'Wendy' is the variety most widely grown.

Perhaps one of the most useful of all grey-leaved edging plants is the favourite catmint, *Nepeta mussinii,* with its aromatic foliage and long succession of lilac-purple flowers. The common form, about 1½ feet tall, is dwarfed by the 3 feet 'Six Hills' variety; there is another, *violacea,* whose flowers are a deep violet.

The *artemisia* species, which include both perennial and shrubby forms, provide a wealth of silver and grey planting material. 'Lambrook Silver', a silken-silvered form of the common wormwood, *Artemisia absinthium,* is widely grown for this colouring but many other species include in their ranks varieties with finely-cut foliage of silver, white or grey, including *A. palmeri,* with a silvery sheen to its leaves, and the white and woolly, willow-leaved *A. ludoviciana,* of which 'Silver Queen' is an outstanding form.

Of the shrubby species, *A. abrotanum,* known to country folk under such names as Southernwood, Lad's love and Old Man, is probably the best-known and most widely-grown. This plant used to occupy a prominent place in almost every cottage garden. Its foliage, however, has only a faint tinge of grey and it is probably grown more for the distinctive, lemony fragrance given off by its feathery foliage when it is crushed.

A. arborescens is one of the finest of all grey-leaved shrubs but unfortunately, it is not completely hardy in the colder districts of the British Isles and will usually need the shelter of a south wall with additional protection in winter. Its finely-divided foliage is reminiscent of silver filigree.

The majestic grey-green foliage of the cardoon, *Cynara cardunculus,* has earned it a well-deserved promotion from the kitchen garden to a position of importance at the back of the herbaceous border. It is now acclaimed as one of the finest of herbaceous perennials and its finely-cut leaves, often 3 feet in length, are greatly valued by flower arrangers.

In summer the thick grey stems of the cardoon are topped with large purple thistle-heads, very much like a more prickly version of those of the globe artichoke. Another stately grey-leaved six-footer for the back of the border is the plume poppy, *Macleaya cordata.* Its beautifully lobed, blue-grey leaves are thickly silvered on their undersides. These rather overshadow the feathery, pinkish-buff inflorescences, although the latter are attractive enough to furnish this perennial with its popular name.

We tend to forget that many kinds of dianthus are grey-leaved plants that serve a decorative purpose even when out of flower. 'Blue Hills', with purple flowers, 'Dubarry', rose-pink, 'John Page', cyclamen and 'Whitehills', flesh-pink, all have compact cushions of silver foliage that makes them interesting plants for all seasons.

The hawkweeds, most commonly encountered as lawn weeds, have several species in which silver foliage plays an interesting part. *Hieracium lanatum* (syn. *H. waldstetnii*), is one of the loveliest of silver-leaved perennials whose downy rosettes have a lasting attraction. It grows from 1¾-2 feet tall but there is also a more compact species, *H. villosum,* suitable for edging or the rock garden, which does not exceed 12 inches.

There are many interesting shrubs in the grey and silver category, and as most of them are evergreen—or ever-grey—they retain much of their beauty throughout

Elaeagnus can be preserved in glycerine solution. Leaves change to pleasant hues of brown and tan

Many silver leaved plants will dry well and can be used in dried flower arrangements

1 *Elaeagnus pungens aureo-variegata* has gold-splashed leaves
2 *Elaeagnus pungens,* the type, will grow to 15 feet. It is a useful shrub, though not so handsome as its variegated leaf varieties
3 *Hosta fortunei marginato-alba*
4 Hostas are useful plants to grow in light shade

the whole year although the colour and texture of the foliage tends to deteriorate during winter, particularly in towns and industrial areas.

Lavender must be the most widely-grown of all grey-leaved shrubs. Primarily, however, it is cultivated for its fragrant flower spikes just as rosemary, another shrub with grey-green leaves, is grown mainly for its culinary uses.

'Folgate', with soft lavender flowers and 'Hidcote', the deepest of purples, are two fine grey-leaved lavenders for all-round purposes, but where foliage alone is concerned, it would be hard to better *Lavandula vera,* the Dutch lavender, which is noteworthy for its broader silvered leaves.

The so-called cotton lavender has this silvery colouring to a much more marked degree. *Santolina chamaecyparissus* is the most distinctives species, its close-packed leaf spikes thickly-felted with silver. It grows to about 1½ feet, but there is a dwarf variety, *nana,* which is better suited for edging or the rock garden.

S. neapolitana is taller than either of these; its foliage, too, is more finely-divided, like the lavenders, santolinas are inclined to legginess, but unlike the lavenders, they do not object to hard cutting back and plants can be pruned to within an inch or two of ground level in spring to provide shapely cushions of silver.

The New Zealand members of the senecio genus, relations of our native groundsel, include a number of sun-loving, silver-leaved shrubs.

Most grey-leaved plants have a preference for light, well-drained soils, but the Sea buckthorn, *Hippophae rhamnoides,* is exceptional in thriving even in semi-bog conditions. This is an attractive-looking shrub that often attains tree-like dimensions. The leaves are slender and willow-like and female plants have clusters of bright orange berries in autumn.

If we exclude conifers, of which there are many with glaucous or silvery foliage, there are not many silver or grey-leaved trees suitable for the average garden. They could be numbered on the fingers of one hand and the weeping pear, *Pyrus salicifolia pendula* is the most attractive of them all. It is distinguished not only for its unusual silvery leaf colouring and form—unusual, that is, for a member of the pear family, but also for the weeping habit that sets the seal on its elegant appearance.

Although normally silvered only on their undersides, the leaves of the whitebeams, especially when in motion, create an impression of dazzling silvery-white. *Sorbus aria,* the common whitebeam, is one of our most attractive native trees.

The species includes a number of outstanding varieties such as *S. a. chrysophylla,* in which the upper surface of the leaves is yellow and *lutescens,* covered with a creamy-white felting. *S. a. pendula* (syn. *salicifolia*), is an interesting narrow-leaved variety with leaves of silvery-grey.

The lists that follow should form a useful blueprint for anyone wishing to plan a garden or border entirely to these unusual and beautiful plants.

Trees *Cedrus atlantica glauca, Populus alba pyramidalis, Pyrus salicifolia pendula, Sorbus aria* varieties.

Shrubs *Amelanchier laevis villosa, Artemisia* species, *Atriplex halimus, Ballota pseudodictamnus, Berberis temolaica, Caryopteris clandonensis, Cistus* species, *Convolvulus cneorum, Eucalyptus* species, *Halimocistus* varieties, *Hebe* species and varieties, *Helichrysum* species, *Hippophae rhamnoides, Lavandula* species, *Olearia* species, *Perovskia atriplicifolia, Phlomis* species, *Potentilla fruticosa* varieties, *Romneya* species, *Salix lanata.*

Herbaceous plants *Anaphalis triplinervis, Artemisia* species, *Centaurea* species, *Convolvulus mauritanicus, Cynara cardunculus, Echinops ritro, Eryngium* species, *Helichrysum* species, *Hieracium lanatum, Lychnis coronaria, Macleaya cordata, Onopordon acanthium, Phlomis* species, *Salvia argentea, Santolina* species, *Stachys lanata, Verbascum bombyciferum.*

CHAPTER NINETEEN
GREEN FLOWERS

Green flower arrangements are very popular with women. Their harmonies are soft and kind. They suit all settings. Yet only comparatively lately have the hybridists given us green flowers. Some of the most striking of these come from bulbs and corms. There are wonderful green lilies to be found listed in catalogues.

Lily hybrids

In recent years the much-improved forms and colours of the highly concentrated and specialised breeding programme of the world-famous lily-breeder, Jan de Graaf, of Oregon, USA, has begun to make an impact on the amateur. Hundreds and thousands of crosses between species and the resulting seedling hybrids have now evolved separate hybrid strains which are continually being improved upon.

But it is better to err on the side of exposure to full sun than to plant the bulbs in full shade. On very limey soils a really generous supply of organic matter is also essential, and if you have very poor, shallow soil in your garden you may find it better to grow lilies in containers rather than in the open ground.

If you are unable to get bulbs early enough for late summer or autumn planting out of doors then plant them in the spring, storing them indoors in trays, covering them lightly with moist peat so

1

2

You can force some kinds of lilies into flower with gentle warmth so that they bloom by Easter

Pot lilies in spring for general summer and autumn flowering. If space is restricted in a greenhouse you can start them off in a cool frame

3

4

1 **The grey-green leaves of**
Ballota pseudo-dictamnus
2 **Lilium 'Green Dragon' is one of the beautiful modern lilies known as Olympic Hybrids, bred in Oregon, U.S.A. It is not a difficult bulb to grow, provided the soil is well-drained**
3 ***Daphne laureola*, the Spurge Laurel, is a native moorland shrub**
4 ***Moluccella laevis*, Bells of Ireland**
5 **'Christabel' a half-hardy *G. Tristis* hybrid with *G. virescens* (syn. *G. bicolor*) is characterised by strong day scent**

5

that their scales and roots remain plump.

Flower arrangements like gladioli which come in such useful shapes! There is the lovely species *G. tristis* as well as green hybrids like the favourite Green Woodpecker. Flowering dates are dependent upon choice of varieties, time of planting, site, and the season's weather. Gladioli are excellent for introducing height to an herbaceous border, as the foliage is tall even before the spikes emerge. They can also be planted in clumps in their own beds, with the smaller cultivars on the perimeters, or in rows in the vegetable garden for cut-flowers. Their range of colour and colour combinations is one of the widest in horticulture.

Some tulips are green or have green in their petals, especially the parrot varieties.

A great favourite of mine, once known as *Iris tuberosa*, is hermodactylus.

Hermodactylus Snakeshead iris. A genus of a single species, similar to bulbous iris, which now grows wild in this country, but originated in the Mediterranean area. Once known as *Iris tuberosa*, *H. tuberosus* grows to 9–12 inches. Its flowers are borne singly on upright stems, and are violet, black and green in colour. They appear from March to May, according to district. **Cultivation** No special conditions are required but an over-moist site should be avoided. The plant increases naturally but slowly by a spreading habit. It can be divided while dormant or raised from collected seed.

The spurges, or euphorbias, have great garden value. They include annual, biennial and perennial herbaceous plants, shrubs and trees and succulent plants. The decorative parts are really bracts, often colourful, round the small and inconspicuous flowers.

Hardy *E. biglandulosa,* 2 feet, yellow, February and March, Greece. *E. cyparissias,* cypress spurge, ploughman's mignonette, 1–2 feet, small narrow leaves, small greenish-yellow flowers and yellow, heart-shaped bracts, May, Europe. *E. epithymoides* (Syn. *E. polychroma*), cushion spurge, 1–1½ feet, rounded heads of golden-yellow bracts, early April to late May, Europe. *E. griffithii,* 1½–2 feet, reddish-orange flowers and bracts, April and early May; the cultivar 'Fireglow' has redder flower-heads, Himalaya. *E. heterophylla,* Mexican fire plant, annual poinsettia, 2 feet, scarlet bracts, annual, North and South America. *E. lathyrus,* caper spurge,

3 feet, large green bracts, biennial, Europe. *E. marginata,* snow-on-the-mountain, 2 feet, leaves banded white, bracts white, annual, North America. *E. myrsinites,* trailing, good when sprouting between stones of a dry wall, fleshy stems, blue-grey foliage, bright yellow flower-heads, late winter and spring, south Europe. *E. pilosa,* 18 inches, usually grown in its form *major,* with yellow foliage, turning bronze in autumn, Europe, north Asia. *E. portlandica,* 9 inches, blue-green leaves, yellow bracts, British native. *E. robbiae,* 1½ feet, rosettes of dark green leaves, bracts yellow, good ground cover plant for shade. *E. sikkimensis,* 2–3 feet, young shoots

bright red, bracts yellow-green, summer, India. *E. veneta* (syn. *E. wulfenii*), to 4 feet, nearly 3 feet across, very handsome almost sub-shrubby plant, grey-green foliage, yellow-green flower-heads with black 'eyes', spring to summer, Europe. Other species and varieties of hardy spurges may be found in nurserymen's catalogues.

Hardy species Any good garden soil suits them. *E. veneta* (*E. wulfenii*) prefers a slightly sheltered position, but the others should be given sunny places. The annuals and the biennial, *E. lathyrus,* are easily raised from seed sown out of doors in April where the plants are to flower, thinning the seedlings later. *E. lathyrus* seeds itself freely.

Given time all flower arrangers admire hellebores.

Cultivation A well-drained rich soil is best and although a shaded position is usually recommended, this is not essential, although partial shade is preferable to full sun. Once established, the plants like to be left undisturbed, although they quickly settle down if they are moved in winter with plenty of soil round their roots. Plant in October, November or March, 15 inches apart in groups, preparing the site well and incorporating some manure.

Propagate from seed or by division of roots after flowering.

There are also many delightful annuals, nicotiana, zinnias, African marigolds and the striking *Molucella laevis* among them.

These flowers are also very useful for winter decoration as they dry well. The 'flowers' have a papery appearance and

1 *Euphorbia epithymoides* makes a colourful spring bedding plant
2 'Green Woodpecker' a gladiolus popular with arrangers
3 *Polygonatum multiforum,* 'Solomon's Seal', or 'David's Harp' produces bell-like white flowers in June
4 *Helleborus x nigricors,* a pale-green flowered hybrid, is slightly perfumed
5 *Euphorbia veneta,* formerly *Euphorbia wulfenii,* is one of the most attractive of herbaceous spurges
6 *Helleborus lividus,* only hardy in sheltered spots and has numerous bell-like flowers that turn brown
7 Nicotiana 'Lime green' is a modern cultivar, popular with flower arrangers, and grows to 2½ feet

All euphorbias exude a milky latex when the stems are cut which can burn the skin and eyes. Wash the hands after handling

To ensure that euphorbias and hellebores take water well, stand the stem ends in an inch of boiling water until it cools and then give them a deep drink in fresh but tepid water

are green and look like shells, hence the name shell flower or bells of Ireland. The flowers are arranged in whorls along the flowering stem.

Species cultivated *M. laevis*, 1½ feet.

Cultivation Moluccellas do best in a sandy loam soil and a sunny position. They should be treated as half-hardy annuals, sowing the seed in heat in February or March. The seedlings are then pricked off and hardened off, ready for planting out in May.

CHAPTER TWENTY
DECORATIVE SEED HEADS

Many of our garden plants give us double value, for they produce decorative seed-heads and fruits as well as flowers or foliage. Some like physalis are grown for these alone.

Cultivation The hardy species require a rich, well-drained soil in a sunny or partially shaded position and should be planted in the spring. The fruits, popularly called 'lanterns' (the inflated calyces) can be picked and dried in the autumn. If left out of doors, they become skeletonised. *P. alkekengi* grows very vigorously and spreads by means of underground runners.

It may be used as a deciduous ground cover plant in sun or semi-shade. Where it is suited it can become something of a nuisance, difficult to eradicate unless every piece of root is removed.

The teasel is another.

Dipsacus cultivation Chalky, well-drained soils in open sunny situations are best. Propagation is from seed sown in the open in May or June, the seedlings thinned and later transplanted to their permanent positions in September for flowering the following year. No staking is required, but the plants need plenty of room and should

be set not less than 2 feet apart. The flower heads should be cut with long stems any time in the late autumn.

In my own garden I grow **lunaria** as a ground cover.

Cultivation *L. annua* needs the standard treatment for biennials, and the final planting positions may be lightly shaded, though they will grow in full sun. Plants make quite large specimens and their lower leaves in particular are large and coarse, so that they should be given ample room. They should be planted at least 1 foot apart.

You can grow gourds just as you would marrows. The small ornamental gourds for indoor decoration belong to the species *Cucurbita pepo,* var. *ovifera.* Seeds are either supplied in mixed packets or in particular varieties according to shape. A good mixture produces gourds in the shape of 'apples', 'pears', 'oranges', 'hardheads', and other odd shapes. They vary in colour from dark green to light yellow and white. Many are beautifully striped, some are heavily warted. The Chinese or

1

2

3

Harvest gourds when they are ripe and before the frosts arrive. Cut each with an inch of stem. Lay them in a warm room to complete the ripening process for two weeks

Honesty planted among spring flowering bulbs will hide their flowers and foliage when they have faded

turban gourds are small and orange-red in colour.

Among the annuals you can find the prettily shaped seed vessels of nigella and poppy.

1 Ornamental gourds produce fruit of widely varying shape and size

2 *Nigella damascena* gets its name Love-in-a-Mist, from the way the leaves surround the flowers

3 *Dipsacus sylvestris,* the native common teasel, will grow to 6 feet

4 The Bladder Cherry, or Chinese Lantern, plant, *Physalis alkekengi,* has bright orange, air-filled papery calyces

5 A decorative relative of the onion, *Allium albopilosum* is a hardy bulb

6 The papery seed heads of Honesty or Moneywort, *Lunaria annua,* persist through the winter and are useful for decoration

5

4

6

CHAPTER TWENTY ONE

FLOWERS TO DRY

Winter arrangements can be fresh. A good gardener should have plenty of plants which provide a succession of branches, leaves and flowers. But even so it helps to have a good supply of dried materials on hand. One great advantage of these is that they stand up well to centrally heated atmospheres.

Everlasting flowers

The natural everlasting flowers are those with papery petals, often called immortelles. The most common are helichrysums and other members of the daisy family including helipterum, ammobium, anaphalis and xeranthemum. A packet of seeds can produce a lovely selection. The sea lavenders are often called statice, but belong to the genus *Limonium*, and they include the two annuals, *L. sinuatum*, in various colours and *L. suworowii*, bright rose, and the perennial *L. latifolium,* with tiny blue flowers.

Cultivation and harvesting All these plants revel in a hot dry summer and last much better after a good season. Sow them in the greenhouse in March to get an early start, planting them out in May. Or sow in the open ground in the sunniest spot in the garden in late April and May, thinning the seedlings to 6 inches apart, and hope for a

1 *Amaranthus caudatus,* Love-lies-Bleeding, a half-hardy annual used to provide foliage and flower colour in sub-tropical bedding schemes
2 *Achillea filipendulina* 'Gold Plate'
3 The silvery-white foliage and chaffy flowers of *Anaphalis nubigena*
4 The purple form of *Gomphrena globosa,* the Globe Amaranth from India
5 The flowers of *Eryngium oliverianum* are surrounded by blue floral bracts
6 Echinops, a good border plant

Flowers for drying must be at the right stage of maturity; if too young they will droop and if too old they will lose their colours

Make flowers into very small bunches. Air must circulate well. Tie them tightly because stems shrink on drying

dry summer.

These flowers for drying need to be cut just as they come to maturity. If they are left two or three days too long the petals are less closely folded over one another and they soon shatter once they are completely dry. Cut them all with stems as long as possible, except perhaps the helichrysums, which often have lateral flower buds. These can be snipped off just behind the head and later given false stems. Tie them loosely in small bunches and suspend them from a cord or wire stretched across a garage or spare room or spread them out on wire mesh frames where there is no dampness and no direct sun. The former will encourage rotting and the latter will bleach the colour away from the flowers. The stems of many flowers bend and are not strong enough to hold the heads. False stems can be made with florist's wire, straws, pipe cleaners or twigs.

Other plants which will dry There are other plants which will retain their colour and shape well after drying and which

4

5

6

associate happily in arrangements with the true immortelles.

Spanish clover, *Gomphrena globosa,* is not so well known.

Species cultivated *G. globosa,* the globe amaranth, from India, a plant 1–1½ feet tall, seed of which is available either in mixed colours or in selected colours including orange-yellow, purple, rose and white. There is also a dwarf form *nana,* 6 inches high, of which 'Buddy' is a purple-flowered cultivar, and seed of a form with variegated leaves is also offered.

Cultivation Sow seed in warmth, either in spring or autumn, and transplant the seedlings to small pots when they are about 1 inch high. Pot on as required in a compost of loam, leafmould and well-decayed manure in equal proportions, with a good sprinkling of sand added. Water regularly and give a liquid feed weekly until the plants flower, always keeping them as near the light as possible. Plants will flower between April and September according to the time of sowing. Cut the flowers as soon as they have developed fully and hang them up to dry.

Both *Amaranthus caudatus,* or love-lies-bleeding and *A. hypochondriacus,* prince's feather, will dry.

Amarantnus

They are good for pot culture under glass. *A. caudatus,* love-lies-bleeding, and *A. hypochondriacus,* prince's feather, are two of the hardiest and can be treated as hardy annuals in warmer areas.

Cultivation Plant out in June in sunny beds. Propagate by seed sown in a temperature of 55–60°F (13–16°C) in March. Harden off young plants carefully before planting out.

Delphiniums and larkspurs or annual varieties need to be dried quickly and out of light. An airing cupboard is a good place.

Gather catananche or Cupid's dart just before the flowers are fully open. Dry quickly in an airing cupboard and they will keep their colour

Some rose buds will dry well. Gather them just as the calyx is beginning to grow away from the petals

Cultivation Sow annual varieties in a sunny, open border in April where they are to flower, or in boxes of light soil under glass in March in a temperature of 55°F (13°C). Prick out seedlings when large enough to handle and transplant in the open in May. Perennials should be planted out in the spring or autumn in beds of rich, deeply cultivated soil; dwarf varieties are suitable for rock gardens. Feed with liquid manure in the early summer. Lift and replant every third year. Propagation of perennial varieties is by means of cuttings of young shoots in early spring, inserted in sandy soil in pots in a shaded propagating frame, or by seeds sown in the open ground in late spring or under glass in spring. *Achillea filipendulina* 'Gold Plate', and 'Coronation Gold', sea holly (*Eryngium*), thistles, teasels, the lanterns of *Physalis franchetii, Moluccella laevis*, (bells of Ireland), echinops, ferns, grasses, gourds, montbretias, cornflowers, heathers, astrantias, lavenders, edelweiss and hops can all be preserved and used, provided they are cut just at the point of maturity and not left too long. Most of these can be dried in the same way as the true everlasting flowers, or laid on sheets of newspaper away from the sun, dampness or heat for a week or two until they are thoroughly dehydrated. Ferns benefit from pressing between sheets of paper under the carpet, or between sheets of blotting paper under a cool iron.

Drying leaves Leaves to accompany this material can be either copper beech, gathered just before they begin to dry, or green beech once it has assumed its golden autumn colour. Put the sprays of leaves into a tall container filled with a mixture of half water and half glycerine, keep them out of direct sunlight until the leaves are silky and then press them under the carpet between sheets of newspaper.

Some leaves, especially the leathery ones such as holly, magnolia, rubber plant (*Ficus elastica*) and camellia, can be skeletonised by leaving them in a tub of rainwater until the outer parts of the leaves become slimy and can be rubbed away, leaving the framework of the leaf. This needs washing in clean water and drying on paper and can be encouraged to curl without breaking once it is quite dry.

All this material, together with the seed-heads of such plants as nigella, columbines, larkspurs, poppies, *Iris foetidissima*, (the gladdon iris) with its brilliant orange fruits, honesty (*Lunaria*) which needs to have the outer coats gently removed to reveal the silvery 'moons' between, the fluffy seed-heads of clematis, the cones of conifers, acorns, nuts and the old female catkins of the alder and other hedgerow or garden material, provides endless scope for dried arrangements for indoor decoration. Materials should be stored in boxes once they have been dried, until they are needed, otherwise they will gather dust and lose their fresh look.

1 *Ammobium alatum,* the Winged Everlasting, is an Australian plant
2 The delphinium border in Regent's Park
3 *Limonium sinuatum* is a useful annual to grow for dried flower arrangements
4 Helichrysums provide many gaily-coloured flowers for winter use

CHAPTER TWENTY TWO
FLOWERS TO CUT FROM BULBS, CORMS AND TUBERS

Naturally, what every woman wants most from a garden is a continuous supply of flowers for cutting, to arrange and to give away.

Cut flowers

One of the greatest joys of a garden is that with a little planning the gardener can have plenty of flowers and foliage for indoor decoration at all times of the year.

Even when done carefully, repeated cutting from the borders robs the garden of much of its decorative value. It is wise to grow plants just for cutting and any odd corner of the garden can be used for this but the best plan is to grow them in rows in the vegetable garden where they will get plenty of light, and the hoe can be worked around them when the vegetables are hoed. Annuals, perennials, ornamental gourds, grasses and even wild plants can be grown to provide material.

How to grow suitable materials Plant perennials 2–3 feet apart to allow the plants to develop well and divide the clumps when they get either too congested or bare in the middle. In general they benefit from a spring mulch of compost. Sow annuals in April or May in rows 9 inches apart and thin them to 6–8 inches apart according to the size of the ultimate plant. The thinnings can always be transplanted, either to some other part of the garden or to make another row for cutting. The hardy annuals, such as asters and sweet peas, and perennials treated as annuals, such as antirrhinums, which need special treatment, should not be forgotten.

Biennials are grown from seed sown in rows in May and thinned in the same way

Wait until daffodils and all other narcissi move from the straight 'pencil' stage to the 'goose neck' development before picking the buds

If you have found that flowers wilt inexplicably after arrangement, try putting them into lukewarm water to harden them

as annuals, but later in the year the plants are best if they are transplanted. This makes them stockier plants, less likely to run to early flower, although the flower arranger might enjoy having Siberian wallflowers or honesty in September.

What to grow Try to vary the annuals, biennials and vegetable material and plants for drying each year so that there can be a constant change of design in flower arrangement from year to year as well as from season to season. Seedmen's catalogues provide many ideas and recommendations and usually indicate the new strains of annual flowers which are always worth trying for a colour break or better constitution.

If some perennials fail, try others better suited to the position or if pyrethrums, especially the double varieties, give disappointing results change to another variety because some of them seem to be very fussy about their surroundings.

When to cut A general rule is not to cut material during the heat of the day but to collect it in the early morning or evening. Evening is perhaps the better time, when the flowers can be given a long drink in a cool place overnight and arranged the following day. Some material such as *Achillea millefolium* will flag when cut during the warm part of the day.

Most flowers need to be cut in bud if they are to last. This applies particularly to tulips, daffodils, paeonies, poppies, iris, roses, and most annuals. Kniphofias (red hot pokers), lupins and antirrhinums need cutting before the flowers at the bottom of the spike begin to fade, they will then curl a little in water and continue to be attractive until all the flowers are open, frequently dropping the older flowers; but the flower dropping is considerably reduced if the spikes are taken from the plant early enough. Lavender, statice, helichrysums and other 'everlasting' flowers, grasses and flowering-heads of such plants as cardoon and artichoke need to be cut before they are fully open. They can be dried by hanging them in small bunches upside down in an airy, cool shed or garage.

1 Dahlia 'Comet', an anemone-flowered type which is becoming popular
2 The De Caen Anemones make splendid cut flowers
These decorative relatives of the onion, *Allium pulchellum* 3, and *Allium moly* 4 are hardy bulbs
5 Dahlia 'Lady Tweedsmuir', a small-flowered Decorative, with blooms over 4 inches in diameter but not exceeding 6 inches

1

If they are dried in the sun they lose their colour and become brittle. Often the stems once dried are inadequate and have to be wired or replaced by tougher stems. Seed-heads and skeletons of *Umbelliferae* and the fluffy heads of clematis need little or no drying if collected after flowering, especially if the plants have been well ripened by the weather.

Cutting It is the treatment the plant material receives at the time of cutting that determines whether it is going to last as long as possible or not in water. Naturally, some flowers do not last well whatever treatment is given and almost no material lasts quite as long once it has been cut as it would if left on the plant.

Always make a good clean cut when taking material from the plant, using scissors, secateurs or a sharp knife. In a very few instances, for example bergenia and heuchera, the stems should be pulled from the plant. There are special flower cutting scissors which have double blades, the one cutting the stem and the other gripping it at the base. These are extremely useful when one hand is holding aside other plants, for with the one hand the stem can be cut from the plant and carried back to the box or basket in which material is being collected without the bloom falling and getting bruised.

If the weather is particularly warm it is worth taking a bucket of water to the plants and plunging the stems into this as soon as they are cut. This is essential for plants such as bergamot and calthas. Hollow-stemmed plants such as delphiniums should have their stems blocked by the thumb the moment they are cut and the hand not removed until it is below the water in the bucket. Further, delphinium spikes, once cut can be turned upside down and the stems filled with water from a jug, plugged with cotton wool and then put into the bucket of water.

Every year I plant a row of poppy

2

3

Flowers last longer in metal containers, for the metal inhibits bacterial activity and so keeps the water sweet

Fresh flowers which have flagged can be quickly revived. Stand their ends in an inch or two of boiling water. Leave until cool, then rearrange

anemones.

The tubers of the popular florists' anemones, varieties of *A. coronaria,* which are excellent cut flowers, together with other tuberous species, may be planted in October and November, or February and March, 3 inches deep, 6 inches apart. Tubers of these may be lifted and stored after their foliage has died down, and kept in a cool place until replanted. Choose a well-drained sheltered spot, previously well manured.

Closely related to these and just as showy are the Asiatic ranunculus. The Asiatic tuberous species need a rich soil, preferably containing one third part of decayed manure. The tubers (usually offered by bulb growers as *Ranunculus asiaticus grandiflorus,* or *R. grandiflora*) are planted 'claws' down, from October or November until April; those described as 'Persian' ranunculus are best planted in late February. All kinds should be planted 2 inches deep and 3–4 inches apart. They are often grown in rows 6 inches apart, for cutting purposes. Apply liquid manure once a week from the time the leaves are seen and water freely if the weather is at all dry. When the flowering season is over the tubers must be sun dried and stored until planting time comes round again.

The handsome seedheads of *Allium albopilosum* were described in the previous section. There are other species whose flowers are delightful and long lasting. Study a bulb catalogue for these.

Outdoor cultivation is very easy. Alliums require only ordinary, well-drained garden soil; most thrive in full sun. They may be used in flower borders, shrubberies or rock gardens. Plant in October or November, at a depth equal to twice the diameter of the bulbs. Increase in spring by small bulbs or seed planted in gritty soil and well fed.

Amaryllis Really gorgeous and somehow so unexpected at the end of summer are these belladonna lilies.

Cultivation Though these plants are regarded as hardy, the site usually chosen for them is in full sun, the foot of a south-facing wall being ideal. This protection is not essential in mild areas. The soil should be well drained and enriched with leaf-mould or well-rotted cow manure. Plant bulbs in June–July, 9 inches deep, 12 inches apart. Established bulbs should be watered freely while in active growth. Mulch annually with manure, while dormant. Bulbs increase naturally and if required for planting elsewhere may be lifted and divided while dormant.

Gladioli We dealt briefly with gladioli in the section on green flowers, so now a little

1 'Homespun', a semi-cactus dahlia
2 'Rotterdam', a medium-flowered semi-cactus dahlia which has blooms over 6 inches in diameter but not usually exceeding 8 inches
3 *Amaryllis belladonna,* the Belladonna Lily, from South Africa, hardy outdoors in warm places
4 Gladiolus 'Weltwunder' grown to exhibition standard
5 The white flowers and golden stamens of *Lilium candidum*

5

more about these useful blooms.

Some species can be grown satisfactorily out of doors in England, especially in the south and west.

Other species are occasionally grown as cool house plants for flowering in March and April. They include *G. alatus*, 1 foot, orchid-flowered, strongly day-scented, scarlet and yellow. *G. blandus*, 1–1½ feet, white, often flushed pink, red lip-markings, unscented. *G. carinatus*, violet and cream, strongly day-scented. *G. grandis*, variable in height, brown or orange flowers, night-scented. *G. tristis*, 1½ feet, creamy-white, night-scented of carnation.

Half-hardy types raised from *G. tristis*, *G. cardinalis* and *G. blandus*, called 'Nanus' and 'Colvillii', will survive the winter outside in the south and flower in May and June.

Cultivation Summer-flowering gladioli may be had in bloom outdoors from late June until the frosts of October.

Two main types are officially recognized: the primulinus hybrids, which have short, slender, but strong and whippy stems, elongated buds, flowers in which the top segment of the perianth regularly forms a hood over the anthers and stigma, airily spaced flowers in 'stepladder' fashion with little or no overlapping and a tendency to face outwards; and the non-primulinus hybrids, with thicker, longer, straight stems, more bulbous buds set closer together, wide-open flowers facing forwards and overlapping to present a gapless ribbon of bloom.

Gladioli will grow in most garden and allotment soils found in Britain, but attention to their specific requirements will be repaid by better spikes and fewer losses. The soil should be balanced and either neutral or slightly acid, the site must receive full sun for most of the day, the larger-flowering types need plenty of nourishment and continuously available water at the roots (but not water-logged conditions), and the corm needs to sit in a fast-draining pocket of light soil or sand. Soils not already rich in organic food should have plenty of old manure, garden compost, or other balanced fertiliser incorporated in the second spit down. A dusting of boneflour or bonemeal on top of the second spit will help root development. The top spit should be kept light and open, as a preventive against corm and neck rots.

Planting depth will vary according to the nature of the soil; but on average soils large corms can be covered by 4–5 inches of soil, the medium-sized ones by 3 inches, and smalls and cormlets by 1½–2 inches. Plant when the soil has warmed up, in late

1 The Golden-rayed Mountain Lily, *Lilium auratum* (Div 7), is sweetly scented
2 The flaring star-shaped flowers of Lilium 'Bright Star' (Div 6d) are shining white with a golden central star
3 *Galtonia candicans,* the Spire Lily, is a bulbous plant from South Africa
4 The white trumpets of *Lilium regale* (Div 9) an easy species to grow
5 A popular South African plant, *Ornithogalum lacteum,* is known as the Chincherinchee and is long-lasting when cut

March and throughout April. For later blooms, plant during May. Use a trowel, not a dibber; place a handful of sharp sand into the bottom of the hole, press the corm firmly into this, and sprinkle some more sand over the top before returning the soil into the hole. Plant the corms at least

6 inches apart (1 foot for exhibition purposes) and leave 9 inches between rows.

What a luxury it seems to have lilies to cut! Yet these flowers are quite easy to grow.

Lily bulbs have no outer protective envelope as have tulips and narcissi, and

Often pot culture for lilies can be the answer to the problem of difficult soils such as very light chalky or sandy types or very heavy clay

All-peat composts are especially suited to pot lily culture. In any case some liquid feeding should be given during active growth and flowering

3

4

5

so tightly packed scales which often serve as a means of multiplying more expensive varieties you may occasionally buy. Long exposure to air dries the bulbs and insects can get between the scales and damage them. If they are allowed to stand in water too long they may rot, so that they should be planted in soil, whether in the open garden or in pots. If the bulbs must be kept out of the ground or out of their pots store them in trays, covered with moist peat or a mixture of moist peat and sand.

When preparing the soil out of doors, mix in plenty of compost, leafmould, or other organic matter, plus some well-rotted manure if you can get it, and plenty of gritty material to provide sharp drainage.

One method of growing lilies on heavy soils is to make raised beds surrounded with logs. Fill in with a load of grit, and then build up a bed of good organically rich soil on top of the grit.

Refuse to buy bulbs which have had their roots trimmed off because the roots are vital in establishing the bulb quickly. They also pull the bulb down to its correct depth—so planting depth need not be adhered to very accurately.

Stem-rooting types also produce roots above the bulb, but these perish when the flowering spikes wither down to ground level. But they largely take over during active growth and flowering. All lilies appreciate monthly liquid feeding during their most active above-ground growing period. Maxicrop and Phostrogen are particularly good for this purpose.

Dahlias are wonderful value for money, and so long as you do not intend to exhibit perfect blooms they are fairly simple to grow.

Cultivation Nowadays dahlias are comparatively easy to grow. They tolerate all soils between the moderately acid and alkaline and for ordinary garden purposes need little or no specialised attention, yet will flower profusely. In their evolution they have produced multiple types and hundreds of thousands of varieties simply because they are a cross-pollinated plant. This means that it is possible to produce unusual and original cultivars by raising plants from seed, which is an additional asset. Furthermore, with correct culture, plants will flower continuously from July until the first autumn frosts, providing a colourful display over a range of several months.

The dahlia plant itself, which provides a type of stock commonly sold by dahlia nurseries, is formed by rooting dahlia cuttings. Plants grown from cuttings flower later than those grown from tubers, though if you need early flowers before mid-August, it is a good idea to specify on the order sheet 'April Delivery'. If you have a greenhouse or frame, you can then pot the plants into 5 inch pots and they will grow into fine bushy specimens by planting out time. This is standard technique for large and giant-flowered varieties.

You cannot plant unprotected dahlia plants out of doors until late May, or even safer, the first ten days in June. With cloches or in sheltered situations, free from late spring frosts, you can plant out in late April or early May. In the north and in Scotland, mid-June.

Planting Out This stage is best tackled by taking out a hole in the ground with a small spade. Stakes should be inserted at this time to avoid damage to the tubers which would occur if they were put in later. The hole should be wide enough to prevent cramping and deep enough to allow the upper surfaces of the tubers to be about 2 inches below ground level. Replace the earth on top, shaking the tuber to settle it round the root as you proceed, firming it in by gentle treading. This applies to both ground and pot tubers. Planting distances are 2 feet apart for pompons, 2½ feet for ball dahlias and all others, except the large and giant decoratives, such as cactus and semi-cactus, which should be 3 feet apart.

Keep the soil watered periodically to swell the tubers and to start the shoots into growth. Shoots should emerge above the soil within five weeks; if not, dig up the tuber and inspect it for decay and slug damage. Slug pellets applied above soil level round the root when planting both tubers and plants are an advisable precau-

tion. Dahlia plants are placed in a hole taken out with a trowel and their roots set so that the potting soil is just below ground level. Bituminised paper, or fibre pots, should be carefully removed from the plants before planting out. (With peat pots especially, make sure to keep the soil moist enough to encourage the roots to penetrate into the open ground, since failure to do this is a frequent cause of stunted, poorly growing plants).

1 The lily-flowered tulip 'Dyanito' has reflexed, pointed petals
2 The white-flowered cottage tulip 'Carrara', a tall-growing kind
3 Parrot tulip 'Estella Rijnveld', a pink-and-red-flowered variety
4 The turban or Persian Buttercup, *Ranunculus asiaticus,* can be had in a range of bright colours
5 Double tulip 'Peach Blossom', a short-stemmed variety

A Recommended List of Bulbs

Early Spring (February–March)

Botanical Name	Common Name	Botanical Name	Common Name	Botanical Name	Common Name
Camassia	Quamash	*Iris reticulata*	Iris	Tulipa	Tulip
Chionodoxa	Glory of the Snow	*Iris danfordiae*		(Species tulips)	
Crocus	Crocus	*Leucojum vernum*	Spring Snowflake	*T. kaufmanniana*	
Eranthis	Winter Aconite	Narcissus		*T. fosteriana*	
Galanthus	Snowdrop	cyclamineus		*T. greigii*	
Ipheion uniflorum		*Scilla sibirica*	Siberian Squill		

Mid-season (March–April)

Hyacinthus	Hyacinths	Narcissus	Daffodil	Tulipa	Tulip
Muscari	Grape Hyacinth	Medium Cupped		Double Early	
Narcissus	Daffodil	Tulipa	Tulip	Triumph	
Trumpet		Single Early		Mendel	

Late (April–May)

Iris (Dutch)	Iris	Tulipa	Tulip	Tulipa	Tulip
Narcissus	Daffodil	Lily-flowered		Darwin Hybrid	
Short Cupped		Double Late		Parrot	
Scilla campanulata	Spanish Squill	Paeony-		Cottage	
		flowered		Darwin	

Summer (June–September)

Acidanthera	Abyssinian	Galtonia	Spire Lily	*Ornithogalum*	Chincherinchee
	Wildflower	Gladiolus	Gladiolus	*thyrsoides*	
Anemone	Windflower	Iris	Iris	Ranunculus	
Begonia	Begonia	English		Sparaxis	African Harlequin
Brodiaea		Spanish			Flower
Crinum	Cape Lily	Ismene		Tigridia	Shell Flower
Crocosmia		*Leucojum aestivum*	Summer Snowflake	*Vallota speciosa*	Scarborough Lily
Dahlia	Dahlia	Lilium	Lily	Zantedeschia	Arum Lily
Freesia	Freesia	Montbretia	Montbretia		

Autumn (September–November)

Crocus (some)	Crocus	Sternbergia	Winter Daffodil	*Zephyranthes*	Flower of the
Colchicum	Autumn Crocus			*candida*	West Wind

Rock Garden

Chionodoxa	Glory of the Snow	Galanthus	Snowdrop	Narcissus	Daffodil
Crocus	Crocus	*Ipheion uniflorum*		Dwarf Species	
Erythronium	Dog's Tooth	Iris	Iris	*Scilla sibirica*	Siberian Squill
dens-canis	Violet	Dwarf Species		*Sternbergia lutea*	Winter Daffodil
Fritillaria		Muscari	Grape Hyacinth	Tulipa Species	Tulip
Dwarf Species					

Naturalising

Anemone blanda		*Endymion*	Bluebell	Leujocum	Snowflake
Camassia	Quamash	*nonscriptus*		Muscari	Grape Hyacinth
Colchicum	Autumn Crocus	Eranthis	Winter Aconite	Narcissus	Daffodil
Crocus	Crocus	*Erythronium*	Dog's Tooth Violet	*Ornithogalum*	Star of
spring and		*dens-canis*		*umbellatum*	Bethlehem
autumn-		*Fritillaria*	Chequered Lily	*Puschkinia*	Striped Squill
flowering		*meleagris*		*libanotica*	
		Galanthus	Snowdrop	*Scilla sibirica*	Siberian Squill

Cut Flowers

Alstroemeria	Peruvian Lily	Iris	Iris	*Ornithogalum*	Star of
Anemone	Windflower	Spanish		*umbellatum*	Bethlehem
De Caen		English		*arabicum*	
St. Brigid, etc.		Lilium	Lily	*pyramidale*	
Convallaria	Lily-of-the	Montbretia	Montbretia	Ranunculus	
majalis	Valley	Muscari	Grape Hyacinth	Scilla	Squill
Crocus	Crocus	*Narcissus triandrus*		Tulipa	Tulip
chrysanthus		*N. cyclamineus*		Taller Species	
Dahlia	Dahlia	*N. jonquilla*		all tall-	
Freesia	Freesia	Doubles		stemmed garden	
Gladiolus	Gladiolus	Trumpet		tulips	
Iris	Iris	Small Cupped		Tritonia	
Dutch		*N. poeticus*		Ixia	African Corn Lily

Indoor Cultivation

Chionodoxa		Hyacinthus	Hyacinths	Narcissus	Daffodil
sardensis		Prepared		types and	
Crocus	Crocus	Early Romans		varieties as listed	
Eranthis cilicica		*Iris reticulata*	Iris	for cut flowers	
Freesia	Freesia	*I. danfordiae*		*Scilla sibirica*	Siberian Squill
		I. histriodes		Tulipa	Tulip
		major		Single early	
				Double Early	

4

5

CHAPTER TWENTY THREE

FLOWERS TO CUT
ANNUALS AND PERENNIALS

So many annuals are wonderful plants for flower arrangement, real cut and come again flowers. I particularly like marigolds, China asters, annual chrysanthemums, all bright and endearing daisies.

Annuals

Hardy annuals are easy to grow and will give a quick and brilliant display provided they are grown in an open, sunny position in any good garden soil. Many annuals are tender and easily killed by frost, so these kinds are sown under glass in the spring and planted out when all danger of frost is over. Some hardy and half-hardy kinds make excellent pot plants for the greenhouse and there are others that need greenhouse cultivation entirely.

Some, such as the nasturtium, flower better if grown on rather poor soil. Most annuals will make too much leaf growth if grown in soil that is too rich or in shady places. Their rapid growth makes them invaluable for the new garden when flowers are wanted the first year, or for filling in gaps in newly-planted herbaceous borders.

Apart from removing faded flowers, keeping them weeded and staking the taller kinds they need little attention.

Growing hardy annuals The soil should be broken down to a fine tilth and well firmed before the seeds are sown. Sow in shallow drills or scatter the seed broadcast after previously marking out the position for each group of annuals selected. Cover the seeds in the drills by drawing the soil

1 *Calendulas,* sometimes called marigolds, are hardy annuals growing 12 to 15 inches in height. The many cultivars include the strain known as 'Art Shades', of which 1 is an example. These are a vast improvement over those with single blooms
2 Various colour forms of the China aster, *Callistephus chinensis.* These half-hardy annuals will flourish in most soils, in open sunny positions
3 *Chrysanthemum segetum,* the hardy annual that grows 12 to 15 inches in height
4 *Scabiosa caucasica* 'Sarah Cramphorn'
5 A fine form of Scabiosa caucasica
6 *Lychnis gothago,* the corn-cockle, is one of many easily grown hardy annuals
7 Erigeron 'Foerster's Liebling' is a semi-double form growing to 18 inches

Some annuals have handsome, decorative foliage. These include the castor oil plant, orach, ruby chard and the dusty millers, or Centaurea candidissima and Cineraria maritima

If you are short of canes support floppy annuals by making a tent of large mesh wire netting for them to grow through

over them, or rake in the seeds sown broadcast. It may be necessary to protect the seeds and seedlings from birds and cats by placing wire netting or brushwood over the seed bed.

Some hardy annuals may be sown in August or September to flower early the following summer out of doors. As soon as the seedlings are large enough to handle they should be thinned. With autumn-sown annuals leave the final thinning until the following spring. Distances apart vary considerably, depending on the ultimate height of the annual, but as a general guide dwarf-growing annuals should be thinned to 4–6 inches apart. Those that grow to 15–18 inches tall should be thinned to 9–12 inches and taller kinds should be thinned to 1–2 feet apart.

Half-hardy annuals Some annuals and a few perennials treated as annuals will not stand frost, so they are sown under glass in pots, pans or seed boxes, using John Innes seed compost or a soil-less seed compost. Sow the seeds thinly and cover and then place a sheet of glass and a piece of brown paper over the pot or box. Turn the glass daily to prevent condensation drips from falling on to the soil. Remove the paper as soon as the seeds germinate but leave the glass on for a further few days, tilting it slightly to admit some air.

When the seedlings are large enough

prick them out into boxes of John Innes potting compost or a soil-less potting compost and shade them for a day or two from strong sunlight.

When watering seed boxes it is best to immerse them in water up to their rims until all the compost is thoroughly damp, i.e., when the surface has darkened. This method is preferable to watering overhead. Where a soil-less seed compost based on peat and sand is used the initial watering usually suffices.

It is essential to harden the plants off well before they are planted out into their flowering positions at the end of May or the beginning of June. Transfer the boxes to a cold frame and gradually increase the

ventilation, eventually leaving the lights off altogether except on nights when frost is likely. If a frame is not available, gradually increase the greenhouse ventilation, finally leaving doors and vents open day and night.

It is a great mistake to sow too early under glass as this simply means that the plants receive a severe check by becoming over-crowded in their boxes while waiting to be planted out into their permanent positions.

The damping-off disease at the seedling stage can be troublesome but it can be controlled to a very large extent by using sterilised compost such as the John Innes or soil-less composts and by watering with Cheshunt compound.

It is also possible to sow half-hardy annuals in the open ground in May or early June and, flowering later, they extend the flowering season.

Greenhouse annuals Many hardy, half-hardy and tender annuals make colourful plants for the cool greenhouse. They may also be grown in this way for cut flowers; or the pots, when in flower, may be taken into the house.

Seed is sown as for half-hardy annuals in pans, pots or boxes and the seedlings are potted up when they are large enough to handle. Pot-on as soon as the roots fill the pot. Some annuals resent being transplanted so it is best to sow these straight into their flowering pots and thin out the seedlings later.

The great advantage of a greenhouse for annuals is that flowers may be had throughout the year by sowing at different times. The temperature when sowing should be about 65°F (18°C), but it is not necessary to maintain this high temperature afterwards provided the greenhouse is completely frost free. Many of the greenhouse annuals will need their growing points pinching out to encourage bushy plants and some will need staking. Water liberally in the summer months but moderately in the winter, and feed the plants with weak liquid manure at regular intervals.

China asters or callistephus offer a pretty range of colours for those who like soft pinks, rose and purples.

Callistephus (kal-is-tef-us)
The original plants had single purple flowers on 2 foot stems but *C. chinensis* has been greatly hybridised to give a wide variety of flower form, in which the petals may be quilled, shaggy, plumed or neat. Colours range from white through pinks and reds to purples and blues and recently yellow has been introduced; heights vary from 6 inches to 2½ feet. Among the most

important are the wilt-resistant strains bred in this country and the USA. These important are the wilt-resistant strains bred in this country and the USA. These flowers may be used for exhibition, bedding, cut-flowers and some strains make useful pot plants.

Cultivation China asters grow on a wide range of soils provided they have been well cultivated and manured and the lime content maintained. Open sunny sites give best results. Seed is sown in March in a temperature of 55°F (13°C), and the seedlings subsequently pricked out and hardened off, for planting out in May. Seed

may also be sown later (April) in the cold frame. Plant out 6–12 inches apart according to the height of the variety. When flower buds show give a feed of weak liquid manure. Never allow the plants to receive a check in any way. When raising plants keep them growing the whole time.

Another self-coloured, aster-like flower is erigeron.

Erigeron (er-ij-er-on)
Hardy herbaceous, daisy-flowered perennials some of which continue to flower intermittently throughout the summer.
Cultivars include: 'B. Ladhams', 1½ feet, bright rose; 'Bressingham Strain', (*E. aurantiacus*), 1–1½ feet, orange to yellow shades, May to July; 'Charity', 2 feet, pale pink; 'Darkest of All', 2 feet, deep violet; 'Dignity', 2 feet, mauve-blue; 'Felicity', 1½–2 feet, deep pink, large; 'Foerster's Liebling', 1½ feet, deep pink, semi-double; 'Gartenmeister Walther', 2 feet, soft pink; 'Merstham Glory', 2 feet, deep lavender-blue, semi-double; 'Prosperity', 2 feet, deep blue; 'Quakeress', 2 feet, pale blue overlaid silvery pink; 'Quakeress White', 2 feet, white; 'Unity', 2 feet, bright pink; 'Vanity', 3 feet, clear pink, late flowering; 'Wupperthal', 2 feet, pale blue.
Cultivation Plant in the autumn or early spring in a sunny position ordinary soil.

Cut down stems after flowering. Named varieties are propagated by division of the clumps in the autumn or spring, the species by seed sown in the open in light soil in a shady position from April to June.

If you have limy soil you will be able to grow lovely **scabious**.
Cultivation These plants all do well in chalky or limy soil, which, however, should be enriched. *S. caucasica* is suitable for the herbaceous border, but may also be grown to supply cut flowers, for which purpose its long clean stems make it very suitable. These plants should be lifted and divided every three or four years, moving them in spring as disturbance in autumn can kill them.
Perennial species cultivated *S. arvensis* (syn. *Knautia arvensis*), field scabious, 1 foot, flowers bluish-lilac, July–August, *S. caucasica*, 1–1½ feet, flowers mauve, blue or white, June to October, Caucasus; vars. 'Clive Greaves', flowers mauve, large; 'Miss Willmott', large, white; 'Moonstone', large, lavender-blue.
Annual species cultivated *S. atropurpurea*, sweet scabious, mournful widow, pincushion flower, 2–3 feet, flowers deep crimson to purple, July to September, south-eastern Europe; cultivars include 'Azure Fairy', blue; 'Blue Moon', pale blue; 'Black Prince', very dark purple; 'Cherry Red'; 'Cockade Mixed', large almost conical flowers in various colours; 'Coral Moon', light to dark salmon; 'Fire King', scarlet; 'Lovliness', salmon-rose; 'Parma Violet'; 'Peach Blossom', pale rose; 'Rosette', deep rose and salmon; 'Snowball', white.

1 *Tropaeolum majus* is the well known and deservedly popular nasturtium of which there are numerous colour forms
2 *Thelesperma burridgeanum,* a hardy annual from Texas, has yellow blooms with reddish-brown centres

A Selection of Hardy Annuals

Botanical Name	Common Name	Height inches	Colour
Althaea	Annual Hollyhock	48–60	various
Anagallis linifolia	Pimpernel	6	blue, red
Argemone	Prickly Poppy	24	yellow, orange, white
Calendula officinalis	Pot Marigold	24	orange, yellow
Centaurea cyanus	Cornflower	12–30	various
Centaurea moschata	Sweet Sultan	18–24	various
Chrysanthemum carinatum	Tricoloured Chrysanthemum	24	various
Chrysanthemum coronarium	Crown Daisy	12–24	various
Clarkia elegans	Clarkia	18–24	various
Collinsia	—	12–15	various
Convolvulus tricolor	Annual Convolvulus	12–18	various
Delphinium ajacis	Larkspur	24–36	pink, red, blue, white
Dianthus sinensis	Indian Pink	6–9	various
Eschscholzia	Californian Poppy	12	various
Gilia × hybrids	—	3–6	various
Godetia	Godetia	6–30	pink, crimson, white
Gypsophila elegans	Annual Gypsophila	18	white, pink, carmine
Helianthus annuus	Sunflower	36–96	yellow, bronze, brown
Helipterum	Everlasting	12	white, pink, yellow
Lathyrus odoratus	Sweet Pea	cl	various
Laverata trimestris	Mallow	24–36	white, pink
Leptosyne stillmanii	—	18	golden-yellow
Limnanthes douglasii	Butter and Eggs	6	white and yellow
Linaria maroccana	Annual Toadflax	9–15	various
Linum grandiflorum	Annual Flax	15–18	red, blue, pink, white
Lobularia	Sweet Alison	3–12	white, pink, lilac
Lupinus hartwegii	Annual Lupine	12–36	various
Malcolmia maritima	Virginia Stock	6–12	various
Malope grandiflorum	Mallow	24–36	pink, crimson, white
Matthiola bicornis	Night-scented Stock	12	lilac
Mentzelia lindleyi	Blazing Star	18	yellow
Nemophila menziesii	Baby Blue-eyes	tr	blue
Nigella damascena	Love-in-a-mist	18	blue, pink, white
Papaver rhoeas	Shirley Poppy	18–24	various
Papaver somniferum	Opium Poppy	18–36	various
Phacelia campanularia	—	9	blue
Reseda odorata	Mignonette	12–18	red, yellow, white
Rhodanthe manglesii	Everlasting	12	rose and white
Salvia horminum	—	18	blue
Saponaria vaccaria	Annual Soapwort	30	pink, white
Scabiosa atropurpurea	Sweet Scabious	18–36	various
Silene pendula	Annual Catchfly	6	various
Thelesperma burridgeanum	—	18	yellow, red-brown
Tropaeolum majus	Nasturtium	6 & tr	oranges, yellow, red
Tropaeolum peregrinum	Canary Creeper	cl	yellow
Viscaria oculata	Catchfly	6–12	various

Hardy Annuals to Sow in the Autumn

Calendula officinalis	Pot Marigold	24	orange yellow
Centaurea cyanus	Cornflower	12–30	various
Cladanthus arabicus	—	30	yellow
Clarkia elegans	Clarkia	18–24	various
Delphinium ajacis	Larkspur	24–36	pink, red, blue, white
Eschscholzia	Californian Poppy	12	various
Godetia	Godetia	6–30	pink, crimson, white
Gypsophila elegans	Annual Gypsophila	18	white, pink, carmine
Iberis	Candytuft	6–15	various
Lathyrus odoratus	Sweet Pea	cl	various
Limnanthes douglasii	Butter and Eggs	6	white and yellow
Lobularia maritima	Sweet Alison	12	white, pink, lilac
Lychnis githago (syn. Agrostemma githago)	Corn-cockle	24–36	pale lilac
Malcolmia maritima	Virginia Stock	6–12	various
Nigella damascena	Love-in-a-mist	18	blue, pink, white
Oenthera biennis	Evening Primrose	30	yellow
Papaver rhoeas	Shirley Poppy	18–24	various
Saponaria vaccaria	Annual Soap-wort	30	pink, white
Scabiosa atropurpurea	Sweet Scabious	18–36	various
Specularia speculum-veneris	Venus's Looking Glass	9	blue
Viscaria	Catchfly	6–12	various

A Selection of Half-Hardy Annuals

Ageratum	Ageratum, Floss Flower	6–18	blue
Amaranthus caudatus	Love-lies-bleeding	24	reddish-purple
*Antirrhinum	Snapdragon	9–36	various
Arctotis hybrids	African Daisy	12–18	various
Begonia semperflorens	Begonia	6–9	white, pink, crimson

(continued from first column)

Botanical Name	Common Name	Height inches	Colour
Brachycome iberidifolia	Swan River Daisy	15	white, pink, blue
Callistephus	Annual or China Aster	9–30	various
Celosia cristata	Cockscomb	12–18	yellow, scarlet
*Cobaea scandens	Cups and Saucers	cl	purple and green
Cosmos bipinnatus	—	36–48	various
Cosmos sulphureus	—	18	orange
Dimorphotheca aurantiaca	Cape Marigold, Star of the Veldt	12–18	orange, buff, salmon, white
Eccremocarpus scaber	Chilean Glory Flower	cl	orange-scarlet
Ipomoea purpurea	Morning Glory	cl	various
Kochia scoparia trichophila	Summer Cypress	12–36	foliage scarlet in autumn
Limonium bonduellii	Annual Statice	12–18	yellow
Limonium suworowii	Annual Statice	18–24	bright rose-pink
Lobelia erinus	Lobelia	6	blue, red, white
Matthiola incana	Ten-week Stock	12–15	various
Mesembryanthemum criniflorum	Livingstone Daisy	tr	various
Mimulus tigrinus	Annual Musk	12	various
Nemesia strumosa	—	9–12	various
Nicotiana	Flowering Tobacco	15–36	white, reds
Petunia	Petunia	9–18	various
Phlox drummondii	Annual Phlox	9–12	various
Portulaca grandiflora	Sun Plant	3	various
Rudbeckia Tetra Gloriosa	Gloriosa Daisy	36	various
Salpiglossis sinuata	Salpiglossis	12–30	various
Salvia splendens	Scarlet Salvia	9–15	scarlet
Tagetes	French and African Marigolds	6–36	various
Ursinia	—	9–18	various
Venidio-arctotis	—	18–24	various
Venidium fastuosum	—	30	various
Verbena hybrids	—	12	various
Zinnia	Zinnia	9–30	various

Annuals for Cutting

Amaranthus caudatus	Love-lies-bleeding	24	reddish-purple
Arctotis hybrids	African Daisy	12–18	various
Calendula officinalis	Pot Marigold	24	orange yellow
Callistephus	Annual or China Aster	9–30	various
Centaurea cyanus	Cornflower	12–30	various
Chrysanthemum carinatum	Tricoloured Chrysanthemum	24	various
Chrysanthemum coronarium	Crown Daisy	12–24	various
Clarkia elegans	Clarkia	18–24	various
Cosmos bipinnatus	Cosmos	36–48	various
Cosmos sulphureus	Cosmos	18	orange
Delphinium ajacis	Larkspur	24–36	various
Dimorphotheca	Cape Marigold	12–18	orange, salmon
Gypsophila elegans	Annual Gypsophila	18	white, pink, carmine
Helichrysum bracteatum	Everlasting	24	various
Lathyrus odoratus	Sweet Pea	cl	various
Matthiola	Stocks	12–15	various
Limonium	Annual Statice	12–14	various
Moluccella laevis	Bells of Ireland	18–30	green and white
Nigella damascena	Love-in-a-mist	18	blue
Phlox drummondii	Annual Phlox	9–12	various
Scabiosa atropurpurea	Pincushion Flower, Sweet Scabious	18–36	various
Tagetes	African and French Marigolds	6–36	various
Tropaeolum majus	Nasturtium	6 & tr	oranges, yellow, red
Zinnia elegans	Zinnia	9–30	various

A Selection of Annuals for the Greenhouse

Ageratum	Ageratum, Floss Flower	6–18	blue
Alonsoa	Mask Flower	12–24	scarlet, pink
Calendula officinalis	Pot Marigold	24	orange, yellow
Celosia cristata	Cockscomb	12–18	yellow, scarlet
Clarkia elegans	Clarkia	18–24	various
Exacum affine	—	12–15	violet, blue
Felicia bergeriana	Kingfisher Daisy	6–9	blue and yellow
Impatiens balsamina	Balsam	24	rose, scarlet, white
Ipomoea purpurea	Morning Glory	cl	various
Mimulus tigrinus	Annual Musk	12	various
Nemesia strumosa	Nemesia	9–12	various
Nicotiana affinis	Flowering Tobacco	15–36	white, reds
Primula malacoides	—	12–18	mauves, pinks
Salpiglossis sinuata	Salpiglossis	12–30	various
Schizanthus	Poor Man's Orchid, Butterfly Flower	12–24	various
Senecio cineraria	Cineraria	18–24	various

cl=climbing   tr=trailing.   *=